Thomas Middleton

Thomas
Middleton

RICHARD HINDRY BARKER

GREENWOOD PRESS, PUBLISHERS
WESTPORT, CONNECTICUT

Library of Congress Cataloging in Publication Data

Barker, Richard Hindry, 1902-1968.
   Thomas Middleton.

      Reprint of the ed. published by Columbia University
Press, New York.
      Includes index.
      1. Middleton, Thomas, d. 1627.
ₜPR2716.B3   1974ₗ   822'.3   74-12880
ISBN 0-8371-7767-7

822.3
M629xb

TO MY MOTHER

Preface

THE following study of Middleton, written nearly fifteen years ago, has been used in manuscript by a few of my former students, and one of them, Professor Samuel Schoenbaum, has paid me the compliment of adopting some of my views. In publishing my study now, I have left out things here and there —a passage on Middleton's style, for example, and some material on authorship—to avoid repeating what Professor Schoenbaum has said in his book on Middleton's tragedies. I have also added a little—especially in the first chapter and the appendix—where recent scholarship has provided me with new information. Still I cannot really say that I have changed my original manuscript very radically.

In my text I have generally confined myself to interpretation, and in my appendix I have given information about editions, dates, sources, authorship, etc.—given it or referred to passages in Chambers and Bentley where it can be found. I have accepted as Middleton's three plays not traditionally assigned to him, *The Revenger's Tragedy*, *The Second Maiden's Tragedy*, and *Wit at Several Weapons*; I have denied him two other plays, *Blurt, Master Constable* and *The Spanish Gipsy*. In every case I have been influenced by my predecessors who have given evidence—or at least made pronouncements—for or against Middleton's authorship. In one case, that of *The Revenger's Tragedy*, I have given new evidence that will, I think, settle the controversy about authorship once and for all. The gist of it is that the strange hero-villain of

The Revenger's Tragedy is not really so very strange but merely the tragic counterpart of the hero in Middleton's comedy, *A Mad World, My Masters*. I scarcely need to elaborate—more at least than I have done on pages 70–71— since the resemblance will be perfectly obvious to anyone familiar with both plays.

On pages 155–56 I have listed the editions from which my quotations are taken, Bullen being the chief one for the traditional works of the Middleton canon. When I have used editions printed from seventeenth-century manuscripts, I have not always reproduced all the eccentricities of punctuation and spelling. My Roman and Arabic numbers separated by periods refer to acts, scenes, and lines of plays (as in II.ii.45); such numbers separated by commas refer to volumes and pages (as in V, 66). In a single case—that of *Wit at Several Weapons*, where the scene divisions are not marked—I have used the Roman numbers for acts and the Arabic numbers for pages (as in III, p. 72).

To the obligations that I have tried to acknowledge in my notes, I should like here to add a very great obligation to Columbia University Press.

R. H. BARKER

Canada Lake, New York
January 31, 1958

Contents

Thomas Middleton

CHAPTER I

Life

IT is remarkable how little we know about the lives of the early English dramatists. We discover from documents—if indeed there are any documents—that they were baptized, that they were married, that they had children; that they owned property, that they went to jail, that they died. We know enough, in short, to be reasonably sure that they existed, but except in rare cases—those of Marlowe and Jonson, for example, where we are fortunate enough to have some of their table talk—we know very little more. We can sometimes make inferences and guesses, especially if their work contains passages that might possibly be autobiographical, but we can never really hope to describe their personalities or to throw much light on the genesis of their art. This is as true of Thomas Middleton as it is of his distinguished contemporary William Shakespeare. We can follow the general outlines of Middleton's career, but we know nothing or next to nothing about the man himself.

A century of intermittent investigation has turned up a number of facts about Middleton's parentage and early life. His father, William Middleton, was a Londoner, a brick-layer who boasted a coat of arms and indeed succeeded in getting a crest for it (a rather odd crest: an ape passant with a collar and gold chain); his mother, Anne Middleton, was the daughter of another Londoner, William Snow.[1] Their

[1] *The Visitations of the County of Surrey Made and Taken in the Years*

marriage, on February 17, 1574, is recorded in the church of
St. Lawrence in the Old Jewry. The same church records the
baptism of their son Thomas, on April 18, 1580, and of their
daughter, Avis or Avice or Alice, on August 3, 1582.[2] The
business of bricklaying presumably went well, for at the time
of his death William Middleton owned or leased two substantial pieces of property. One, in Limehouse, had a "tene-
ment" and a wharf on it. The other, some four acres of land
adjoining the Curtain Theatre and indeed called "the Cur-
teyne garden," had several tenements, some at least built or
rebuilt by the owner himself.[3] William Middleton made his
nuncupative will on January 20, 1586, just a day or two before his death and while indeed he was "lyeinge vppon his
deathe bedd." According to an inventory in the Guild Hall
Record Office, his estate amounted to a little more than £335,
of which a third was to be divided between his children. "And
the mother," says the inventory, "dothe, of her free graunte
make yt vpp C. marks a pece and thone to be the others heir
yf either of them dye wthin age the portion being vnpaid."[4]

Long before the legacies could be paid and in fact less than

1530, 1572, and 1623, ed. W. Bruce Bannerman (London, 1899), p. 188,
also printed, with additional information, in Middleton, *Works,* ed. Alexander Dyce (London, 1840), I, ix–xii.

[2] *The Register of St. Lawrence Jewry, London, 1583–1676.* ed. A. W.
Hughes Clarke (London, 1940), Part I, pp. 17–18, 83, and Mark Eccles,
"Middleton's Birth and Education," *Review of English Studies,* VII (Oc-
tober, 1931), 431–41.

[3] Information in this and subsequent paragraphs about William Middleton's property and the family quarrels about it is taken from Middleton,
The Ghost of Lucrece, ed. Joseph Quincy Adams (New York and London,
1937), pp. xxiv–xxv, note 5; Mildred G. Christian, "Middleton's Residence
at Oxford," *Modern Language Notes,* LXI (February, 1946), 90–91;
Christian, "A Sidelight on the Family History of Thomas Middleton,"
Studies in Philology, XLIV (July, 1947), 490–96; P. G. Phialas, "Middleton's Early Contact with the Law," *Studies in Philology,* LII (April, 1955),
186–94; and Mark Eccles, " 'Thomas Middleton a Poett,' " *Studies in
Philology,* LIV (October, 1957), 516–36.

[4] Middleton, *Ghost of Lucrece,* ed. Adams, pp. xxiv–xxv, note 5.

ten months after her husband's death, Anne Middleton re-married. The step was a rash one, as she herself apparently half realized, for her second husband, a certain Thomas Harvey, was anything but a substantial citizen. He was or aspired to be a grocer, but he had recently gone off with an expedition, organized by Sir Walter Raleigh and led by Sir Richard Grenville, to make his fortune in the New World. The expedition had been a complete failure. Harvey and his companions had spent a dreary year starving and fighting Indians on Roanoke Island, until they had finally been rescued by Sir Francis Drake. Harvey himself had "spent or lost whatsoeu[er] he [had] embarked & shipped in the same fleete for his p[ro]vision & trafficke of Marchandise or otherwise." When he got back to London, he was "poore and vnable to paye his Creditors."[5] Under the circumstances he may well have felt fortunate in getting a wife who owned property, even one with two small children to support. But, as it turned out, he was wrong; the marriage was as rash a step for him as it was for his bride.

Within a short time the Harveys were fighting each other tooth and nail, the issue being the property left by William Middleton and the income it provided. Trickery and chicanery seem to have been accepted as legitimate weapons, sometimes trickery of the rather improbable sort afterwards represented in Thomas Middleton's comedies. Thus in November, 1586—very shortly after the marriage—Harvey was the victim of a particularly ingenious and nasty trick. His wife had herself arrested for the children's share of the property, and to keep from being arrested himself, he had to pay down the whole sum in ready money. This obliged him to "suffer his goodes to be sould at An outcrye at his doore." Three years later he must have been at least holding his own, for the tenants of the Curtain property complained that he was spend-

[5] Christian, "A Sidelight on the Family History of Thomas Middleton."

ing money riotously and leaving next to nothing "for the
relyeffe of his Wieffe & her children." Later still—when he
returned from an absence, "on Her Majesty's service," in
Portugal and the Low Countries—he asked his wife for £30;
but she gave him a mere 50 shillings and indeed got rid of
him again by threatening to have him arrested. In 1595 he
tried to poison her, or so she said, and after being haled into
court again he seems to have given up the fight for several
years and to have stayed abroad, where he was at least safe
from his creditors.

In Harvey's absence the fight—already reaching the pro-
portions of a family feud—went on with another figure, Al-
lan Waterer, as Anne Harvey's principal adversary. Waterer,
described as a cloth-worker of St. Leonard's, Shoreditch, married Thomas Middleton's sister, Avis or Alice, and promptly
collected her share of the inheritance. Then, not finding or
not wanting to find lodgings for his wife, he moved in with
his mother-in-law. The situation was explosive and before
long explosions of some violence began to occur. In the summer of 1598 Waterer sued for a writ of attachment in which
he asked sureties of the peace against Thomas Harvey, Anne
Harvey, Thomas Middleton, and another person indirectly
involved in the family affairs. From this action it would
appear that for the moment Anne Harvey had the upper
hand in the household, but a year later she had so far lost it
that she felt obliged to ask for outside help—that of a certain
Philip Bond. She told Bond that "her sonne Allen Waterer
would and went about to thruste her out of her house: and
forbade her tenantes to paye her any rent." [6] Bond refused to

---

[6] Phialas, "Middleton's Early Contact with the Law." Waterer once said
that his mother-in-law "went about by develishe and subtell practizes . . .
to deceave all the world and then lastlie her owne Children." But Waterer,
who seems to have been somewhat intemperate—he once attacked Harvey
and nearly killed him—cannot be considered altogether trustworthy. See
Eccles, " 'Thomas Middleton a Poett.' "

help her but—"shee seeminge then to be very sycke"—summoned her husband, who had by this time turned up in London again. When Harvey came she confessed, or pretended to confess, the wrongs she had done him, and for a day or two they were reconciled. But soon afterwards, when he came to the house again, she shut the door in his face, and when Bond, who had come along too, rebuked her, she said: "Tis no matter, nowe I have other Counselle to doe soe." Ultimately—on June 10, 1600—Harvey lost patience and started suit to get control of the property, naming in his bill both his wife and Waterer.

It is not clear to what extent young Thomas Middleton was involved in the family feud or how he was affected by the irregularities in his mother's household. He may well have suffered severely, he may have acquired all sorts of complexes, and we should perhaps expect from psychiatrists, when they finally get around to his case, the most sensational revelations. Meanwhile, however, we can only say that he played what appears to have been a minor part in his mother's legal activities and that he was once at least rather hard-pressed for money.

In April, 1598, when he was just eighteen years of age, Middleton was matriculated at Queen's College, Oxford, as *plebei filius*. His signature at Subscription has been found and identified.[7] It is said, in the course of a legal document, that he had a fellowship, obtained for him by Harvey, his stepfather, but this seems unlikely. An ex-grocer living abroad can scarcely have had much influence at Oxford. In any case, Middleton is said in the same document to have lost his fellowship when—at the time of Waterer's action for sureties

---

[7] Eccles, "Middleton's Birth and Education" and " 'Thomas Middleton a Poett.' " In Middleton, *Works*, ed. A. H. Bullen (London, 1885–86), VII, 325, Middleton speaks of Queen's as his college; see Mildred G. Christian, "An Autobiographical Note by Thomas Middleton," *Notes and Queries*, CLXXV (July–December, 1938), 259–60.

of the peace—he returned temporarily to London. He "did come home," the document says, "to ayde his mother againste his brother in lawe in the absence of his Father in Lawe." The extent or success of his aid is unknown, but at some time within the next two years he seems to have reached an understanding with Waterer. Indeed he sold him his half share of the Curtain and Limehouse property in exchange—such are Middleton's words—for money "paid and disbursed for my advauncement & p[re]ferment in the Vniv[er]sity of Oxford where I am nowe a studient and for my maintenance with meat drinke and apparrell and other necessaries." [8]

Nothing is known about Middleton's career at Oxford, but it is possibly significant that, in one of his pamphlets, he tells the story of a young man, obviously very much like himself, who went to the university without the advantages of wealth. The young man traveled, Middleton says, not on horseback but in Hobson's wagon; his wardrobe was small, his books were not above four in number. When he got to Oxford he attached himself, as poor scholar and servant, to a Londoner's son, "a pure cockney," and by this means managed to creep into an old battler's gown.

Now, as for study and books, I had the use of my young master's; for he was all day a courtier in the tennis-court, tossing of balls instead of books, and only holding disputation with the court-keeper how many dozen he was in; and when any friend of his would remember him to his book with this old moth-eaten sentence, *nulla dies sine linea,* True, he would say, I observe it well, for I am no day from the line of the racket-court. Well, in the meantime, I kept his study warm, and sucked the honey of wit from the flowers of Aristotle—steeped my brain in the smart juice of logic, that subtle virtue,—and yet, for all my weighty and substantial arguments, being able indeed to prove anything by logic, I could prove myself never the richer, make the best syl-

[8] Christian, "Middleton's Residence at Oxford."

logism I could: no, although I daily rose before the sun, talked and conversed with midnight, killing many a poor farthing candle, that sometimes was ungently put to death when it might have lived longer, but most times living out the full course and hour, and the snuff dying naturally in his bed.[9]

So he worked, consoling himself with the prospect of future advancement, until

in the spring of all my perfections, in the very pride and glory of all my labours, I was unfruitfully led to the lickerish study of poetry, that sweet honey-poison, that swells a supple scholar with unprofitable sweetness and delicious false conceits, until he burst into extremities and become a poetical almsman, or at the most, one of the Poor Knights of Poetry, worse by odds than one of the Poor Knights of Windsor.

His first effort was an elaborate poem, "dispersed into a quaint volume fairly bound up" and dedicated to a prospective patron named Sir Christopher Clutchfist.

The book he entertained but, I think, for the cover's sake, because it made such a goodly show on the backside: and some two days after, returning for my remuneration, I might espy—O lamentable sight, madam!—my book dismembered very tragically; the cover ript off, I know not for what purpose, and the carnation silk strings pulled out and placed in his Spanish-leather shoes.

Now it happens that before he left Oxford Middleton himself published poems—no fewer than three of them, in fact. One is dedicated to the Earl of Essex and one to the wealthy Lord Compton. It has been suggested that the Sir Christopher of the pamphlet, also described as "the Muse's bad paymaster," is a satirical portrait drawn from life, perhaps a portrait of Lord Compton himself.[10] Such suggestions can

[9] This quotation and those that immediately follow are from the Bullen edition, VIII, 102–8.

[10] Middleton, *Ghost of Lucrece*, ed. Adams, pp. xxiii–xxxi.

scarcely be verified, but it seems certain that the whole passage
reflects the bitterness of a young man whose experience as
student and poet had been anything but happy.

Middleton may perhaps have finished his studies at Oxford
and taken his degree, but there is no evidence that he did so,
and he turns up rather oddly in London during what might
have been the final months of his academic career. In fact on
February 8, 1601, a witness in the family lawsuit says that
"nowe [Middleton] remaynethe heare in London daylie ac-
companinge the players." [11] Accompanying the players—the
phrase is tantalizingly vague, but it seems to mean that he
was doing something more than just seeing plays day after
day. Perhaps he was already writing or trying to write for
the stage. On April 21, 1601—just a few days after his
twenty-first birthday—he collected his share of his father's
estate and presumably turned it over to Waterer. If he did,
he may well have found some other source of income, for
at about this time he was prosperous enough, or rash enough,
to get married.

His wife, Mary Marbeck or Merbeck, came from a family
rather more distinguished than Middleton's own. Her
paternal grandfather, John Marbeck, was a well-known musician—after 1541 organist of St. George's Chapel, Windsor
—and an ardent disciple of Calvin. In 1544 he was tried for
heretical views and sentenced to suffer at the stake. He escaped
—because of his musical talent he was given a royal pardon
just in the nick of time—but not soon enough to avoid a
temporary place in Foxe's *Book of Martyrs*. He subsequently
published the first English concordance to the Bible, as well
as a number of musical and theological works. One of his
sons, Dr. Roger Marbeck, was Provost of Oriel College,
Oxford. He was the university's first public orator for life,
and in this capacity he twice welcomed Queen Elizabeth in

[11] Phialas, "Middleton's Early Contact with the Law."

Latin speeches. He was later chief physician to the Queen and registrar for life of the London College of Physicians. In 1596 he accompanied Lord Howard to Cadiz and wrote an account of the expedition which was later printed in Hakluyt's *Voyages*. He is thought to have been the author of the entertaining *Defense of Tobacco* (1602). Another of the musician's sons, Edward Marbeck, was Mrs. Middleton's father. He was one of the Six Clerks in Chancery. Mrs. Middleton had a brother who was for a time at least an actor with the Admiral's Men, and it is possible that through him she met her future husband, perhaps while he was still accompanying players. Nothing is known about the Middletons' family life except that they had a son, Edward, born in 1603 or 1604, who was still living twenty years later.[12]

The first definite indication that Middleton was writing for the stage occurs in 1602, when his name appears, five times altogether, in Henslowe's diary. He is down for payments in connection with Henslowe's two companies, the Admiral's and the Earl of Worcester's Men. These companies were scarcely the most reputable in London, for though they occasionally and as it were by accident produced distinguished plays—*Doctor Faustus* or *The Shoemaker's Holiday* or *The White Devil*—they specialized in crude and dreary popular entertainment, synthetically prepared. Authors, working singly or in groups, turned out at high speed anything that would bring them in a few pounds and hold an audience for a few days. Their pieces were seldom printed and obviously were seldom considered worth printing. According to Henslowe's entries, Middleton turned out two pieces of this sort for the Admiral's Men. The first was called *Two Shapes* (apparently an alternate title, though a very strange one, for *Caesar's Fall*, also mentioned in the diary); Middleton

[12] *D. N. B.*, articles "John Marbeck or Merbeck" and "Roger Marbeck, Markbeeke, or Merbeck," and Eccles, "Middleton's Birth and Education."

worked on it with Dekker, Drayton, Webster, and Munday, and received a final payment on May 29, 1602. The second, which he wrote alone, was called *The Chester Tragedy* or *Randal Earl of Chester*; on October 21 he received £4 for it and on November 9 an additional £2. On December 14 he received 5 shillings for a prologue and epilogue for a court performance of *Friar Bacon and Friar Bungay*. Meanwhile, he was at least trying to sell something to the Earl of Worcester's Men—a play, as yet unnamed, for which on October 3 he was advanced a pound.[13]

Middleton's work for Henslowe can perhaps be regarded as his apprenticeship, and it was by no means a bad one for a young man fresh from the university and no doubt inclined to be somewhat bookish. In any case, it was short. He was soon working for more reputable companies, the Children of Paul's and the Children of the Chapel—perhaps, indeed, already working for them, since at least one of his plays for the children, *The Family of Love*, can scarcely be dated much later than 1602. The children's companies, made up chiefly or entirely of boys, acting in relatively small indoor theatres—the so-called private houses—and attracting somewhat more cultivated and more aristocratic audiences than those at the Fortune and the Rose, can perhaps best be described as the arts companies of the early seventeenth century. They sponsored a group of highly intellectual young playwrights—mostly university men with literary aspirations—and indeed produced plays that very directly reflected the intellectual currents of the day. If they failed to come up with another *Faustus* or another *Hamlet*, it can certainly be said that they set a high standard with their repertory, and that for a while at least they drew very substantial audiences.

[13] Henslowe, *Diary*, ed. W. W. Greg (London, 1904–8), I, 166, 167, 171, 172, 182; II, 222, 225, 232.

Shakespeare says that they competed successfully with the adult companies, and in the course of half a volume devoted to the subject Professor Harbage has not quite succeeded in demonstrating that Shakespeare was ill informed.[14]

It seems clear that at a very early age—certainly by his twenty-fifth year—Middleton was accepted, along with such men as Chapman, Marston, and Jonson, as one of the principal playwrights of the children's companies. Yet it seems equally clear that he was not writing for them because he had any special fondness for their audience or any special feeling for the dignity of his art. He apparently thought of himself as a purely practical playwright and he was certainly willing to sell his product wherever he could—more often than not, for the time being, to the children's companies, but never only to them. In 1602, as I have suggested above, he was probably working for both the children and Henslowe. Between March, 1603, and April, 1604, when the theatres were closed, he was probably writing *The Phoenix* for the Children of Paul's and at the same time helping Dekker with *The Honest Whore* for the Admiral's—now called Prince Henry's—Men. Meanwhile he was turning out two pamphlets, *The Ant and the Nightingale* and *The Black Book,* and adding a speech to Dekker's *The Magnificent Entertainment,* a pageant written to welcome the new royal family to London. When the theatres reopened he went on writing for the children, chiefly, it seems, the Children of Paul's, for whom, between 1604 and 1606, he did at least three comedies, *Michaelmas Term, A Mad World, My Masters,* and *A Trick to Catch the Old One.* He may well have done *Your Five Gallants* for them too. But during the same period he did at least one play, *The Viper and Her Brood,* for the Children of the Chapel

[14] Alfred Harbage, *Shakespeare and the Rival Traditions* (New York, 1952). The Shakespeare passage is of course the one in *Hamlet,* II.ii.

—now called the Children of the Blackfriars—and he was almost certainly the author of *The Revenger's Tragedy,* acted by the King's Men.

The Viper and Her Brood is known only from a lawsuit which, like many entries in Henslowe's diary, illustrates the odd financial dealings of seventeenth-century dramatists. The plaintiff in the suit was Robert Keysar, Master of the Blackfriars. He maintained that Middleton owed him £16 and indeed that on May 6, 1606, Middleton had entered into a bond to pay him £8 and 10 shillings before June 15. Middleton answered that on the very next day—May 7—he had delivered to Keysar the manuscript of *The Viper and Her Brood,* in full satisfaction of the bond and accepted as such. The answer was no doubt a truthful one, and yet in another case—that of an innkeeper named Hebson, with whom he ran up a debt of no less than £26—Middleton seems to have been rather slow about repayment and perhaps inclined to stop before he quite got to the end. At least some years afterwards—in another lawsuit—the last £7 of the £26 was described as a desperate debt.[15]

After the collapse of the Children of Paul's in 1606 a number of Middleton's plays were published—some of them at least because the company that owned them could now make money from them in no other way. In a prefatory note to one of them Middleton says, or is represented as saying, that the play was in the press before he knew about it—a pretty clear indication that he himself had not peddled the manuscript. There is no evidence that he had anything at all to do with the publication of the other plays or indeed that he thought of his plays as having any literary interest. Four of them—I am including *The Revenger's Tragedy*—were

[15] Harold N. Hillebrand, "Thomas Middleton's *The Viper's Brood,*" *Modern Language Notes,* XLII (January, 1927), 35-38, and Eccles, " 'Thomas Middleton a Poett.' "

published anonymously, two others had his initials on the title-page, and only one had his name, or at least his last name, spelled out. This would scarcely suggest that, in the eyes of booksellers, Thomas Middleton was as yet exactly a name to conjure with. I might add here that, during that last twenty years of Middleton's life, only three more of his plays were published and two of these were written in collaboration. One of them has a signed preface in which Middleton offers his work to the reading public not as art but as venery and laughter—at least sixpence worth of the former and enough of the latter "to keep you in an afternoon from dice at home in your chambers." [16]

At some time between 1606 and 1608, possibly as a result of his quarrel with Keysar, Middleton seems to have abandoned the children and begun offering his plays to the adult companies only. He gave *The Roaring Girl* (which he wrote with Dekker) to Prince Henry's Men and *A Chaste Maid in Cheapside* to the Lady Elizabeth's. In 1611 he gave *The Second Maiden's Tragedy* to the King's and for a decade thereafter he seems to have worked chiefly for this company, the most distinguished and most successful one in London, the company of Shakespeare and Fletcher. Several of his King's plays—*The Witch* and *The Widow*, for example— are rather more in Fletcher's manner than his own, but from his point of view this can scarcely have been a fault. He was deliberately adapting himself to changing tastes and no doubt measuring his success by the number of plays that he sold. As in his twenties he had been one of the principal playwrights of the children, so now in his thirties he established himself as one of the principal playwrights of an even better company, the King's Men.

Middleton was clearly a modest success in the theatre, but since for a seventeenth-century playwright success seldom

[16] Preface to *The Roaring Girl*.

meant wealth, he was obviously glad to get commissions for
other work, even quite routine work, so long as it paid something. His first chance seems to have come in 1613–14, when
he was asked to do an entertainment for the opening of the
New River, a pageant for the Lord Mayor's entry into London, and a masque, called the *Masque of Cupid*, for a
banquet given by the city at the Merchant Taylors' Hall.
Other commissions followed and by 1620 he was probably de-
voting a substantial part of his time to pageant work, most of
it for the City of London.

The entertainment for the opening of the New River, the
first of the pieces written during the winter of 1613–14, was
designed to honor two men by the name of Middleton—Sir
Thomas Middleton, who had just been elected Lord Mayor
of London, and Hugh Middleton, who was just finishing the
construction of a public water system. It was perhaps inevitable that the commission for the piece should have been
given to a third man by the same name. On Michaelmas Day,
1613, the officers of the city gathered at the cistern near
Islington, watched a parade of laborers all dressed in green
caps and all bearing symbols of their employment, then
listened to a short speech praising the public benefactor. As
the flood-gates were opened and the cistern began to fill, the
speaker concluded with the following lines:

> Now for the fruits then: flow forth, precious spring,
> So long and dearly sought for, and now bring
> Comfort to all that love thee; loudly sing,
> And with thy crystal murmur struck together,
> Bid all thy true well-wishers welcome hither!   VII, 266

The piece is of course slight, consisting in fact of little more
than a single speech; but it is not much slighter than *Civitatis
Amor*, written when Charles became Prince of Wales (1616),
than the ten *Honorable Entertainments Composed for the
Service of this Noble City* (1621), or than the *Invention*

for a feast at the Lord Mayor's house (1622). Middleton's entertainments scarcely belong to literature, but they show that when he had to he could turn out the kind of rhetoric that appealed to the city.

The first of the Lord Mayor's shows, *The Triumphs of Truth,* contains besides rhetoric a lavish amount of spectacle, for Middleton, like his predecessors, was hired to provide something for the eye—to design the "pageants" or wagons surmounted by scenery that could be stationed along the line of the Lord Mayor's march and could house the allegorical figures who delivered the speeches. The pageants in *The Triumphs of Truth* were unusually elaborate, partly because the expenses were borne by the wealthy Grocers' Company and partly perhaps because Middleton was anxious to outdo one of his predecessors, Anthony Munday. On the title-page he says that the work was "directed, written, and redeemed into form, from the ignorance of some former times, and their common writer, by Thomas Middleton," and in the first paragraph of the text he goes out of his way to sneer at Munday's achievements.

The show began on the morning of October 29, 1613, when the Lord Mayor, issuing from the Guild Hall, encountered a figure "representing London, attired like a reverend mother, a long white hair naturally flowing on either side of her; on her head a model of steeples and turrets; her habit crimson silk, near to the honourable garment of the city; her left hand holding a key of gold." The Mayor listened to her speech and then passed on to the wharves, where he saw —floating upon the water—"five islands, artfully garnished with all manner of Indian fruit-trees, drugs, spiceries, and the like; the middle island with a fair castle especially beautified." On each of the islands was a figure representing one of the Five Senses and under it an appropriate emblem—an eagle for Sight, a hart for Hearing, a spider for Touch, an ape for

Taste, and a dog for Smell. After going by barge to Westminster and taking the oath of office, the Mayor landed
again at Baynard's Castle, where he was welcomed by two
figures on horseback representing Truth's Angel and Zeal,
one dressed in white silk powdered with gold stars, the other
in flame-colored silk and a bright wig that shot out fire-beams.
The figures accompanied him to Paul's Chain, where in the
south yard he saw

Error in a chariot with his infernal ministers . . . his garment
of ash-colour silk, his head rolled in a cloud, over which stands
an owl, a mole on one shoulder, a bat on the other, all symbols
of blind ignorance and darkness, mists hanging at his eyes. Close
before him rides Envy, his champion, eating of a human heart,
mounted on a rhinoceros, attired in red silk, suitable to the bloodi-
ness of her manners; her left pap bare, where a snake fastens; her
arms half naked; holding in her right hand a dart tincted in blood.

VII, 241

Error spoke temptingly but Zeal forced him back and made
way for another chariot in which Truth herself sat

in a close garment of white satin, which makes her appear thin and
naked, figuring thereby her simplicity and nearness of heart to
those that embrace her; a robe of white silk cast over it, filled
with the eyes of eagles, showing her deep insight and height of
wisdom; over her thrice-sanctified head a milk-white dove, and
on each shoulder one, the sacred emblems of purity, meekness, and
innocency; under her feet serpents, in that she treads down all
subtlety and fraud; her forehead empaled with a diadem of stars,
the witness of her eternal descent; on her breast a pure round
crystal, showing the brightness of her thoughts and actions; a sun
in her right hand, than which nothing is truer; a fan, filled all
with stars, in her left, with which she parts darkness, and strikes
away the vapours of ignorance.   VII, 244

After more speeches the two chariots joined the procession
and the Mayor moved on to Paul's Churchyard, where he

again saw the five islands and near them a ship that seemed to move without sailors or pilot. It contained only four figures —"a king of the Moors, his queen, and two attendants, of their own colour." But the greatest spectacle of all awaited the Mayor near the Little Conduit in Cheapside—

the true form and fashion of a mount triumphant, but the beauty and glory thereof overspread with a thick, sulphurous darkness, it being a fog or mist, raised from Error, enviously to blemish that place which bears the title of London's Triumphant Mount. . . . At the four corners sit four monsters, Error's disciples, on whom hangs part of the mist for their clothing, holding in their hands little thick clubs, coloured like their garments; the names of these four monsters, Barbarism, Ignorance, Impudence, Falsehood. . . .

VII, 250–51

At the command of Truth, the mist suddenly rose and changed

into a bright-spreading canopy, stuck thick with stars, and beams of gold shooting forth round about it, the mount appearing then most rich in beauty and glory, the four monsters falling flat at the foot of the hill: that grave, feminine shape, figuring London, sitting in greatest honour. . . .   VII, 252

About her sat Religion, Liberality, Perfect Love, and other figures, for Middleton was nothing if not allegorical. But it is scarcely necessary to follow the procession farther, or to describe Middleton's later pageants—written between 1617 and 1626—which differ very little from *The Triumphs of Truth* in their general character.[17]

In his pageant work Middleton was apparently what today would be called the director or producer as well as the author. On the title-page of *The Triumphs of Truth* he says that

[17] For further information, see R. C. Bald, "Middleton's Civic Employments," *Modern Philology*, XXXI (August, 1933), 65–78. Also Robert Withington, "The Lord Mayor's Show for 1623," *PMLA*, XXX (March, 1915), 110–15.

he "directed" the performance, and an entry in the accounts of the Grocers' Company—an entry relating to *The Triumphs of Honor and Industry* (1617)—confirms his statement:

Payde to Thomas Middleton, gent. for the ordering, overseeing and writyng of the whole devyse, for the making of the Pageant of Nations, the Iland, the Indian Chariot, the Castle of Fame, tryming the Shipp, with all the several beastes which drew them, and for all the carpenter's work, paynting, guylding and garnysh-ing of them, with all other things necessary for the apparelling and finding of all the personages in the sayd shewes, and for all the portage and carryage, both by land and by water, for the lighters for the shew by water, for paynting of a banner of the Lord Mayor's armes, and also in full for the greenmen, dyvells and fyer works with all thinges thereunto belonging according to his agreement, the sōme of . . . . 282 o o [18]

Middleton, in short, was responsible for the whole under-taking, even though he obviously had, working under him, a number of skilled craftsmen and artists. In 1613 he names three of them—Humphrey Nichols, who made the fireworks, Anthony Munday, who (of all people!) supplied apparel and porters, and John Grinkin, who apparently made the pageants. In 1617 he praises Rowland Bucket, "chief master of the work," as well as his friend Henry Wilde and the painter Jacob Challoner, who were—he says somewhat enigmatically—"partners in the business." But the man he most frequently mentions is the sculptor or "carver," Garret Christmas, who seems to have established himself as the master of pageant design. Middleton's relations with Christmas are far from clear, but it looks as if the two men ultimately formed a part-nership somewhat like that between Ben Jonson and Inigo Jones—the one outlined the allegory and supplied the speeches, the other designed the costumes and scenes. But in

[18] J. B. Heath, *Some Account of the Worshipful Company of Grocers of the City of London* (London, 1854), p. 410.

this case—if one may judge from Middleton's rather casual statements—the partnership was entirely happy, lasting until shortly before Middleton's death.[19]

The first of Middleton's three masques—written, like the entertainment for the opening of the New River and *The Triumphs of Truth*, in the winter of 1613–14—is known only from an entry in the city records directing that Middleton be paid "for all his disbursements and paynes taken by him and others in the last *Mask of Cupid* and other Shewes lately made" at the Merchant Taylors' Hall.[20] The occasion was a city banquet, given on January 4, 1614, for the recently married Earl and Countess of Somerset. "All the meate," says a contemporary observer,

> was serued to the Table, by choyse cittizens of comeliest person- age, in their gownes of rich Foynes, selected out of the 12. hon- orable companies: after supper, & being risen from the Table, these noble guests were entertayned with a Wassaile, 2. seuerall pleasant maskes, & a play, & with other pleasant dances all which being ended, then ye Bride, & Bridegroome wt all ye rest, were inuited to a princely banquet, & about 3. a clock in the morning they returned to white hall.[21]

The *Masque of Cupid* was presumably one of the "2. seuerall pleasant maskes." A later piece of the same type was *The Inner-Temple Masque; or Masque of Heroes*, "presented as an entertainment for many worthy ladies," probably as part of the New Year's festivities in January or February, 1619. *The World Tossed at Tennis*, written in collaboration with Rowley, was intended for a celebration at Somerset House, but it was apparently rejected by the court and sub- sequently given in the theatre by Prince Charles's Men. It

---

[19] For Middleton's references to his associates, see Bullen, VII, 262, 307, 332, 350, 367, 396, 411.

[20] Printed in Dyce, I, xix–xx.

[21] John Stow, *The Annales, or Generall Chronicle of England* (1615), p. 928, reproduced in Dyce, I, xx–xxi.

contains, like *The Inner-Temple Masque,* a good deal of buffoonery which adds—and can at the time have added—very little to Middleton's reputation.

After working on several of the Lord Mayor's shows, Middleton apparently applied for the post of Chronologer to the City of London, a post which was probably intended to include that of Inventor of the City's Honorable Entertainments. On September 6, 1620, the post was granted him with a salary of £6 13s. 4d., which was raised, on January 23, 1621, to £10. But the city records show that he got from time to time additional sums of money—£15 on September 17, 1622, £20 on February 5, 1623, 20 marks on September 2, 1623 (the last "towardes the charges of the service latelie performed by him att the shuting at Bunhill before the Lord Maior and Aldermen and for his service to be performed att the Conduitt heades"). He was also three times given "the nominacion and benefitt of one persone to be made free of this Citty by redempcion"—a benefit that may have been considerable.[22] As Inventor of Entertainments he composed speeches of welcome and interludes for city banquets; as Chronologer he kept a manuscript journal of public events, parts of which were seen by Oldys more than a hundred years later.

They were sold in an Auction of Books at the Apollo Coffee House in Fleet Street abt the year 1735 by Edw Lewis but puffd up to a great price, bought back, & coud not afterwds be recoverd. They are entitled I. *Annales:* or a Continuation of Chronologie; conteyninge Passages and Occurrences proper to the Honnoble Citty of London: Beginninge in the Yeare of our Lorde 1620. By Thomas Midleton then received by their Honnoble Senate as Chronologer for the Cittye. There are in it, these Articles under the year 1621.—On Good Fryday in the Morn died John

---

[22] The records are reproduced in Dyce, I, xxiii–vii; *Analytical Index to the Remembrancia* (London, 1878), p. 305, note; and Bald, "Middleton's Civic Employments."

(King) Lord Bp. of London.—28 May Fra. Ld Verulam committed to the Tower. (Seal taken from him the last day of April).
—27 Decr. Sr Edwd Coke Committed to the Tower.—Decr. The Fortune Play House, situate between White Cross Street and Golding Lane, burnt, &c. II. *Middleton's Farrago:* In which there is—The Earl of Essex his Charge agt Visct. Wimbleton, & the Viscts. Answr.—The Treaty and Articles of Marriage between Pr. Cha: & Hen: Maria.—Parliamentary Matters, 1625–26.— Habeas Corpus 1627 &c.[23]

In the meantime Middleton continued to write plays for the King's Men and occasionally for the Prince's and the Lady Elizabeth's. He collaborated with Rowley in *The Old Law, A Fair Quarrel,* and *The Changeling,* and with Webster in *Anything for a Quiet Life.* He also wrote unassisted *Hengist, King of Kent, Women Beware Women,* and *A Game at Chess.* The last—an atttack on the former Spanish Ambassador, Count Gondomar, and the Spanish party in England— was an unprecedented success at the Globe, but later involved the actors and the author himself in serious difficulties with the government.[24]

A Game at Chess was so well received when it first appeared, on August 6, 1624, that, unlike other new plays in the

[23] Dyce, I, xxiii–iv, note.

[24] See Middleton, *A Game at Chesse,* ed. R. C. Bald (Cambridge, 1929), and G. E. Bentley, *The Jacobean and Caroline Stage* (Oxford, 1941–56), IV, 870–79. More recent information is to be found in Geoffrey Bullough, " 'The Game at Chesse': How It Struck a Contemporary," *Modern Language Review,* XLIX (April, 1954), 156–63, and P. G. Phialas, "An Unpublished Letter about *A Game at Chess,*" *Modern Language Notes,* LXIX (June, 1954), 398–99. From E. M. Albright, *Dramatic Publication in England, 1580–1640* (New York and London, 1927), pp. 196–97, it appears that Middleton had already ridiculed the Spanish Ambassador in *The Triumphs of Honor and Industry,* where there is said to have been a Spaniard who "kept kissing his hands right and left, but especially to the Spanish ambassador . . . in such wise as to elicit roars of laughter from the multitude." In the printed text, however, the Spaniard—presumably the same one—does nothing but offer the Lord Mayor and the grocers good wishes.

Jacobean theatres, it was allowed to run day after day. It was followed, a contemporary observer says,

wth extraordinarie concourse, and frequented by all sorts of people old and younge, rich and poore, masters and servants, papists and puritans, wise men etc. churchmen and statesmen as Sr Henry Wotton, Sr Albert Morton, Sr Beniamin Ruddier, Sr Thomas Lake, and a world besides; the Lady Smith would have gon if she could have persuaded me to go wth her, I am not so sowre or severe but that I wold willingly have attended her, but that I could not sit so long, for we must have ben there before one o'clocke at farthest to find any roome. they counterfeited his [i. e. Gondomar's] person to the life, wth all his graces and faces, and had gotten (they say) a cast sute of his apparell for the purpose, wth his Lytter wherin, the world sayes lackt nothing but a couple of asses to carrie yt, and Sr George Peter, or Sr T. Mathew to beare him companie.[25]

Additional details are supplied by other contemporaries. One says that the actors took in £100 a day. Another—no less a personage than Gondomar's successor, the new Spanish Ambassador—says that the smallest audience during the first four days was over 3,000. He speaks of merriment, hubbub, and applause in the theatre, of spectators emerging so inflamed against Spain that he himself was advised to stay off the streets and see that his house was well guarded—precautions he did not neglect. Meanwhile he was protesting strenuously to the King, demanding either that the persons responsible for the play be punished or that he be given a ship so that he could retire to Flanders. The King and his ministers moved slowly, but after the ninth performance action was finally taken. The theatre was closed; both the actors and the author were ordered to appear before the Privy Council and submit to examination. The actors, who did so on August 18, argued that they themselves were not at

[25] Middleton, *Game at Chesse*, ed. Bald, p. 163.

fault inasmuch as the play had been duly licensed—as indeed it had been—by the Master of the Revels. Nevertheless they were reprimanded and forbidden to act (though, as it turned out, they were permitted to resume acting about ten days later, after they had promised that they would never give the *Game at Chess* again). Middleton, who was more vulnerable than the actors, failed to appear on August 18 and again on August 30, when the Privy Council summoned his son. The chances are that he kept conveniently out of the way until he was quite sure that the official anger had cooled. There is indeed a story to the effect that he was later

committed to prisson where hee lay some Tyme and at last gott oute upon this petition presented to King James

> A harmles game: coyned only for delight
> was playd betwixt the black house and the white
> the white house wan: yet stille the black doth bragge
> they had the power to put mee in the bagge
> use but your royall hand. Twill set mee free
> Tis but removing of a man thats mee.[26]

But stories of this sort usually seem a little too neat to be credible.

Two years after the storm over *A Game at Chess*, Middleton seems to have involved himself in further difficulties, this time with his city employers. It was felt that his pageant for 1626 was "ill" performed, and that a special pageant he and Christmas had prepared to welcome the new King and Queen was hopelessly bad. There were "abuses and badd workmanshipp"—or so the City Records say—"in and about the contrivings and payntings" of the wagons, and as a result neither Middleton nor Christmas seems to have been paid

[26] *Ibid.*, p. 166. Bullough has discovered a version with an additional couplet immediately before the last one:

> And yt wch makes malicios ioy more sweete
> I lye nowe vnder hatches in ye ffleete.

in full. Christmas was ordered to take down the wagons already built, but was allowed to keep the material "for his full satisfaccon." [27] How serious this was—whether or not Middleton had jeopardized his position as Inventor of the City's Honorable Entertainments—it is impossible to say, for eight months later, well before the election of the new Lord Mayor, the dramatist died.

His burial, on July 4, 1627, is recorded in the parish church of Newington Butts, where he is known to have lived as early as 1609. On February 7, 1628, his widow—called Magdalen Middleton and therefore possibly a second wife—petitioned the city for money and received, not as a payment due her husband, but as a gift, the sum of twenty nobles. But if she was left poor, as the petition suggests, she was a burden to the city only until July, when her burial too is recorded in the same parish church. [28]

I have said that Middleton was a successful playwright, and the evidence certainly indicates that for more than twenty years he was able to turn out plays that the theatres found profitable. Still there is nothing to suggest that he had—or indeed that he felt he deserved—a very high reputation as a man of letters. During his lifetime he was never the subject of commendatory verses, and he was never singled out for particular praise in accounts of contemporary authors. It seems clear that he was not, like Chapman and Jonson, a critical success. His work—less pretentious, less learned, and less obviously related to the classics than theirs—was apparently felt to be distinctly popular in character, and it is quite possible that Jonson himself was expressing the general opinion when he said that Middleton, like Markham and Day, "was not of the number of the Faithfull, [i.e.] Poets" and "but

[27] Robert Withington, *English Pageantry* (Cambridge and London, 1918–20), I, 234–35, and Bald, "Middleton's Civic Employments."
[28] Dyce, I, xxxviii–xl.

a base fellow." [29] Shortly after these disparaging remarks
were made, Middleton produced his masterpieces, *The
Changeling* and *Women Beware Women*, but there is no
indication that, in the eyes of his contemporaries, his stature
perceptibly grew. No elegiac verses were addressed to him
when he died, and no folio edition of his works appeared.
There is indeed some evidence that he was still read, by a few
people at least, as late as the middle of the seventeenth
century. He is quoted, with surprising frequency, in John
Cotg.ave's *English Treasury of Wit and Language* (1655),[30]
and he is actually praised in *Wit's Recreations* (1640). "Face-
tious Middleton," says the anonymous author of an epigram
printed in this miscellany,

> Facetious Middleton, thy witty Muse
> Hath pleased all that books or men peruse.
> If any thee dispise, he doth but show
> Antipathy to wit in daring so:
> Thy fam[e]'s above his malice, and 'twill be
> Dispraise enough for him to censure thee.[31]

But neither the quotations nor the praise can, in the absence
of other allusions, be regarded as very significant. For genuine
recognition and certainly for anything like critical attention,
Middleton had to wait nearly two centuries—until the
period of Lamb and Dyce, Bullen and Swinburne. More than
Webster, more than Dekker—more than any other Jacobean
author, in fact—Middleton is the discovery of these critics
and scholars of the nineteenth century. He is a man who made
very little mark upon his own time but was seen long afterwards to be a dramatist of the first or almost the first rank.

[29] Jonson, *Works*, ed. C. H. Herford, Percy and Evelyn Simpson (Oxford, 1925–52), I, 137.
[30] G. E. Bentley, "John Cotgrave's *English Treasury of Wit and Language*
and the Elizabethan Drama," *Studies in Philology*, XL (April, 1943), 197.
[31] Dyce, I, xlix.

CHAPTER II

First Works

MIDDLETON'S first works were written during a period of transition, when the spirit of Elizabethan literature was undergoing a profound change. The romantic tradition—the tradition of Sidney and Spenser—was still very much alive. Euphuism and Arcadianism were still cultivated, sonnets were still written, romantic histories and romantic comedies were still produced at the public theatres. But another tradition, more realistic and more critical, had already succeeded in establishing itself. During the last years of the sixteenth century and the first years of the seventeenth, it had found expression in the pamphlets of Greene and Nashe, in the satires of Hall and Guilpin, in the satirical plays of Marston and Jonson. It was growing stronger and more articulate; it was soon to destroy, or profoundly to modify, the spirit of romance and to produce the dramatic masterpieces of the age—*Hamlet* and *King Lear*, *Volpone* and *The Alchemist*, *The White Devil* and *The Duchess of Malfi*.

Middleton was young enough to feel the full force of this critical tradition, to nourish himself on the younger writers of the age, and to turn to them repeatedly for inspiration. He learned something from Greene, who explored the Elizabethan underworld and described the tricks and swindles of contemporary sharpers; something from Nashe, who exercised his wit at the expense of contemporary folly. He learned something from Marston, who surveyed the corruption

of court life, who dwelt on the nastiness of sex, who adopted
a harsh satirical style and a tangled dramatic structure; something from Jonson, who analyzed the minds of unbalanced
characters. It is sometimes a little difficult, in view of the
uncertain chronology of Elizabethan drama, to determine
the exact extent of his indebtedness, but it is clear that he
was not the first writer in the field, that he attempted the
subjects and imitated the style of men slightly older than
himself, that he expressed—much as they expressed—the
critical spirit of the English Renaissance, which was just then
entering its final phase.

He was young enough to feel the influence of men like
Marston and Jonson, but he was also old enough to be, in
his earliest works, uncertain of his allegiance. He drew at
first on the romantic tradition, he cultivated an ornate and
euphuistic style, he showed at times surprising indifference
to the writers who were changing the literature of the age.
The story of this first episode in his career—of his struggle
to free himself from alien influences—is contained in three
poems, two plays, and two pamphlets, all published by 1608
and all probably written by 1604, a date that can perhaps
be said to mark the end of Middleton's apprenticeship.

I

Of the three poems, two—*The Wisdom of Solomon
Paraphrased* (1597) and *The Ghost of Lucrece* (1600)—
show no traces whatsoever of the critical tradition. They
are exercises in a still fashionable romantic style—exercises
and not much more. The first is a highly rhetorical and ap-
pallingly long-winded paraphrase of *The Wisdom of Solomon*
in the Apocrypha, a paraphrase in which each verse is ex-
panded, embellished, and used as an excuse for a variety of
verbal tricks. The thought is never very important, and it
is sometimes a little difficult to realize that there is any thought

at all. The verse, "I myself also am a mortal man, like to all, and the offspring of him that was first made of the earth," [1] is surely simple enough, but when Middleton gets through with it, it has become almost hopelessly mannered and involved:

> What am I? man; O what is man? O nought!
>   What, am I nought? yes; what? sin and debate:
> Three vices all in one, of one life bought:
>   Man am I not; what then? I am man's hate:
> Yes, man I am; man, because mortal, dead;
> Mortality my guide, by mischief led.
>
> Man, because like to man, man, because born;
>   In birth no man, a child, child, because weak;
> Weak, because weaken'd by ill-fortune's scorn;
>   Scorn'd, because mortal, mortal, in wrong's wreak:
> My father, like myself, did live on earth;
> I, like myself and him, follow his birth.   VIII, 190

And so endlessly and unintelligibly the preposterous exercise proceeds. As one turns the pages one wonders why Middleton bothered to make the work so long, and one wonders too why he bothered to write it at all.

The Ghost of Lucrece is a complaint, somewhat like the complaints made popular by *The Mirror for Magistrates*. The spirit of the Roman heroine rises from the Other World and seems about to begin her tragic story, but in this case the story has already been told by Shakespeare, and Middleton can only draw out her lamentations and embroider them with his intricate and tasteless rhetoric. He borrows freely from Greene's *Ciceronis Amor*, as well as from Shakespeare's *Rape of Lucrece*, but the general effect is scarcely more pleasing than that in *The Wisdom of Solomon Paraphrased*. In a later work Middleton somewhat flippantly describes his performance, or one very much like it, as "an elaborate poetical

[1] It is difficult to tell what version Middleton used, but the sentence cannot in any case have been so very involved.

building—a neat, choice, and curious poem . . . industriously heaped with weighty conceits, precious phrases, and wealthy numbers" (VIII, 107), and the description fits it exactly. A single stanza is quite enough to illustrate the wealth of the conceits and the preciousness of the phrases:

> "Tarquin the Night-owl": Enter Treachery.
> Sextus Tarquinius, this sixth hour is thine.
> Farewell, my life! farewell, my chastity!
> Farewell (though not mine now) that which was mine!
> Thy grapes are now devour'd, alas, poor vine!
>   The Tyr-ant with his force of luxury
>   Tires me an aunt through imbecility.

The third poem, *Micro-Cynicon* (1599), is in its subject matter at least entirely different. It is an attempt at formal satire in the manner of Persius and Juvenal—an attempt presumably inspired by Hall's *Virgidemiarum* (1597-98). Middleton begins—just as Hall begins—with a "Defiance to Envy" and an "Author's Prologue," then goes on to a series of "six snarling satires," each concerned with a different contemporary type. In the first two he deals with the usurer and the prodigal—characters who were soon to play a prominent part in his comedies of London life; in the last four, with the fine lady, the sharper, the "ingle," and the fool. At his best he succeeds in being readable and even lively, as in his description of the prodigal's equipage:

> Suit upon suit, satin too, too base;
> Velvet laid on with gold or silver lace
> A mean man doth become; but he must ride
> In cloth of finèd gold, and by his side
> Two footmen at the least, with choice of steeds,
> Attirèd, when he rides, in gorgeous weeds:
> Zodon must have his chariot gilded o'er;
> And when he triumphs, four bare before
> In pure white satin to usher out his way,
> To make him glorious on his progress-day.   VIII, 121

At his worst he involves himself in all sorts of thorny verbal tangles, notably word-play and antithesis of the most obvious and most detestable sort. But the important thing about *Micro-Cynicon* is not that its style is mannered but that its subject matter is on the whole realistic. It shows Middleton for the first time turning away from romantic masters and trying, though in a medium obviously ill-chosen, to record his impressions of Elizabethan life.

II

Apparently the earliest of Middleton's surviving plays, *The Family of Love*, is perhaps a little closer to *Micro-Cynicon* than to *The Ghost of Lucrece*. It is, superficially at least, another realistic and satirical work. The scene is London, and the characters are such contemporary types as the courtier who carries on amours in the city, the citizen who is jealous of his wife, and the Puritan who is transparently hypocritical. But the realism is never convincing, and there is a good deal in the play that is not realistic at all. There is a balcony scene that comes from *Romeo and Juliet*, there are passages of blank verse that come from *Tamburlaine* and *Hero and Leander*.

> Words cannot force what destiny hath seal'd.
> Who can resist the influence of his stars,
> Or give a reason why 'a loves or hates,
> Since our affections are not rul'd by will,
> But will by our affections? 'Tis blasphemy
> 'Gainst love's most sacred deity, to ask
> Why we do love, since 'tis his only power
> That sways all our affections; all things which be,
> Beasts, birds, men, gods, pay him their fealty.   I.i.14–22

Middleton, in short, is still reluctant to draw on his own experience and still fascinated, perhaps in spite of himself, by the masterpieces of Elizabethan romance. Hence the confused and unsatisfactory impression that the play makes, the mixture of styles, and the disconcerting lapses from realism. Swinburne is scarcely too harsh when he says that *The Family of Love* is "unquestionably and incomparably the worst of Middleton's plays: very coarse, very dull, altogether distasteful and ineffectual." [2]

Romantic and realistic influences are also apparent in *The Phoenix*, possibly written a year or two after *The Family of Love*. But in this case the influences are more completely assimilated; the play has a point of view and a style of its own. It is not quite the mature drama of Middleton, perhaps, but it is certainly not a pastiche of Marston and Shakespeare. It is Middleton's first really distinguished work, his first important contribution to contemporary literature.

The plot is essentially the same as that used in *The Malcontent* and *Measure for Measure*. It is the story of a prince who wanders about his country in disguise, searching for enormities. He finds them—finds enough to satisfy even the most misanthropic reader. He finds monstrously vicious characters who would not be out of place in *The Malcontent* itself or even in *The Revenger's Tragedy*. But he also finds characters who—throughout the greater part of the play at least—seem genially wicked and amiably eccentric, characters who might well have been drawn by the author of *Henry IV*. Prince Phoenix is himself a commentator and judge as well as a busybody. He reflects in long soliloquies the author's views about the vices of Ferrara, and at the end of the play he metes out appropriate punishments.

Of the more odious characters, the worst are certainly the despicable Sea-Captain and the treacherous lord named Proditor. Both are so hopelessly depraved, so utterly repulsive that their actions excite not only disapproval but disgust. Well may Phoenix exclaim:

[2] *Thomas Middleton*, ed. Havelock Ellis, Mermaid Series (London, 1887–90), I, xiv.

What monstrous days are these!
Not only to be vicious most men study,
But in it to be ugly; strive to exceed
Each other in the most deformed deed.   I.iv.267–70

The most striking episode is perhaps the one in which the
Captain—here almost a symbol of unscrupulous greed—arranges to sell his wife, the virtuous and beautiful Castiza. The
terms are fixed, and as the deed of sale is read, the Captain
counts one by one the five hundred crowns he has received.
Phoenix watches and comments—in a bitter apostrophe to
"Reverend and honourable Matrimony"—and when the
transaction is complete, even the purchaser turns on his un-
speakable cuckold:

The baser slave art thou; and so I'll tell her:
I love the pearl thou sold'st, hate thee the seller.
Go to sea; the end of thee—is lousy.   II.ii.231–33

A few minutes later the end comes. Phoenix and his friend
Fidelio throw off their disguises, strip the Captain of his
crowns, and send him into banishment.

Monster, to sea! spit thy abhorred foam
Where it may do least harm; there's air and room;
Thou'rt dangerous in a chamber, virulent venom
Unto a lady's name and her chaste breath.   II.ii.319–22

Another scoundrel, though a somewhat less odious one, is
Tangle, the litigious man, who is always up to his ears in
lawsuits. He lives to vex others, and he has already so beg-
gared his whole parish that "they are not able to spare so
much ready money from a term, as would set up a new
weathercock; the churchwardens are fain to go to law with
the poors' money" (I.iv.146–49). In one scene he advises, or
rather misadvises, two suitors; in another he conducts a kind
of symbolic fencing match with a justice of the peace in which
each thrust and parry represents a different legal trick; in still

another he loses his suits and goes raving mad. But he is ultimately cured by Quieto, a humor of just the opposite sort. The stage business is not fully described, but Quieto seems to go through the motions of bleeding Tangle and so draining off the harsh legal terms—described as blood blacker than ink—that have unsettled his mind. The influence of Ben Jonson is strong in these scenes, especially in the last one, which was obviously suggested by the final episode of Crispinus in *The Poetaster*.

Much more genial than Tangle, and much more amusing, are the Jeweller's Wife and the Knight, two characters who represent in their small way the most influential classes of contemporary society. The Jeweller's Wife wants a "friend" —specifically, a friend at court; the Knight wants money—to pay for his horse and keep his lackey in "steaks" of velvet. Hence their intrigue; hence too their terms of endearment, for while she calls him her "Pleasure," he calls her his "Revenue." In their first scene she proposes to spend the night with him at her father's house, and she goes about it with so much self-assurance and such disarming candor that one forgets to think ill of her, just as one forgets to think ill of Falstaff when he drinks too much sack.

> *Knight.* But do you mean to lie at your father's all night?
> *Jeweller's Wife.* Why should I desire your company else?
> *Knight.* 'S foot, where shall I lie then?
> *Jeweller's Wife.* What an idle question's that! why, do you
> think I cannot make room for you in my father's house as
> well as in my husband's? they're both good for nothing else.
> I.v.29–36

Later in the play she steals a hundred and fifty angels from her husband. But in attempting to deliver the money, she makes a mistake—she gives it to a stranger in the dark—and in the meantime her Pleasure is arrested by catchpolls as he issues, half-drunk, from his tavern. He is rescued, but only

at the last moment, by a drinking companion, who momentar-
ily "blinds" one of the officers and thus makes possible the
escape. The action is always lively enough to have an interest
of its own, but one is never quite allowed to forget that the
author is commenting on the social aspirations of the middle
class and on the extravagance of the impoverished gentry.

If the scenes of the Jeweller's Wife and the Knight are
successful, the scenes involving Falso and his men are a
triumph—one of the greatest triumphs, in fact, in Middleton's early comedy. For Falso is an even more disarming
scoundrel than his daughter, an even more delightful illus-
tration of human weakness.[3] He was in his youth a highway-
man, but now that he is too old for such pleasures he has
become a justice of the peace. Still his contact with the highway has not been entirely lost, for he encourages his men to
ride abroad at least once a quarter and he often dreams of his
romantic past.

I remember [he says] now betimes in a morning, I would
have peeped through the green boughs, and have had the party
presently, and then to ride away finely in fear: 'twas e'en venery
to me, i' faith, the pleasantest course of life! one would think
every woodcock a constable, and every owl an officer. But those
days are past with me; and, a' my troth, I think I am a greater
thief now, and in no danger. I can take my ease, sit in my chair,
look in your faces now, and rob you. . . .   III.i.64–72

And he does—he robs everyone—though as a matter of principle he is quite willing to save a fellow thief, a man who has
robbed a vestry, for example.

What, what? alas, poor knave! Give me the paper. He did but
save the churchwardens a labour: come, come, he has done a
better deed in't than the parish is aware of, to prevent the knaves;

[3] See U. M. Ellis-Fermor, *The Jacobean Drama* (London, 1936), p. 132.
Miss Ellis-Fermor is on doubtful ground only when she says that genial
sympathy is "the essence of [Middleton's] early comic mood."

he robs but seldom, they once a quarter: methinks 'twere a part of good justice to hang 'em at year's end, when they come out of their office, to the true terrifying of all collectors and sidemen.

II.iii.131–38

In the same spirit Falso undertakes to save one of his own men, who has been caught robbing on the highway. He examines the culprit long enough to discover that thieves are valuable members of the commonwealth.

. . . if the whole world were but of one trade, traffic were nothing! if we were all true men, we should be of no trade: what a pitiful world would here be! heaven forbid we should be all true men! Then how should your worship's next suit be made? not a tailor left in the land: of what stuff would you have it made? not a merchant left to deliver it: would your worship go in that suit still? You would ha' more thieves about you than those you have banished, and be glad to call the great ones home again, to destroy the little.   III.i.165–74

He finds the argument entirely convincing, but since justice is demanded, he commits the culprit—with a terrifying display of severity—to the custody of his accomplices, one of whom is at the moment pretending to take down the proceedings, but is actually drawing horse-heads on the parchment.

Falso is so good-natured and so artlessly whimsical that he seems as harmless as one of Shakespeare's comic characters—Dogberry, for example. But in the last act it appears that he is not really harmless after all. He belongs to an evil world, he is part of a group picture which includes such repulsive figures as Proditor and the Captain; and so when the Court assembles and punishments are meted out, when Proditor is banished and the Jeweller's Wife is lectured, Falso must be punished too. He must be deprived of his office and his ill-got wealth—must, as he says, be left "worse than an innkeeper." For the moralistic mood of the serious scenes is clearly the dominant one, and all the offenders, even the most genial of the lot, must in the end be brought to justice.

Middleton's growing maturity is seen, not only in the structure and characterization of *The Phoenix,* but also in its style. There is still word-play no doubt, some of it embedded in the sombre soliloquies of Prince Phoenix, but there is none of the frigid ingenuity, the euphuistic extravagance that mars the poems and even certain pages of *The Family of Love.* The verse is as harsh and bitter as that in *The Revenger's Tragedy;* the prose is as witty and gay as anything in *A Trick to Catch the Old One* or *A Mad World, My Masters.* Middleton had found his medium; as a stylist he had very little to learn.

III

The Phoenix is about half way between the romantic drama of Shakespeare and the satirical drama of Marston and Jonson; the two pamphlets published in 1604—*The Ant and the Nightingale; or Father Hubburd's Tales* and *The Black Book*—are wholly realistic and satirical. They continue the tradition of Nashe and Greene, they deal with contemporary manners, they sketch, in an almost obtrusively witty style, the foibles of contemporary society. It is true that they both have fantastic frameworks—one of them directly borrowed from Nashe's *Pierce Penniless*—but by this time the fantastic framework had become one of the conventions of the Elizabethan satirical pamphlet.

The Ant and the Nightingale begins with a long dialogue in stanzaic verse between Philomel and an ant who has climbed up a tree to admire her, a dialogue in the course of which the author significantly turns aside to condemn euphuism and to apostrophize the genius of Nashe. But the real action gets under way when the author shifts to prose and takes up the first of three case histories, the story of the prodigal heir who dissipates his ancestral estate. The heir is essentially the same character as the Knight in *The Phoenix*, except that here one sees him at the beginning as well as at the end of his career. One follows him step by step—much as one follows the progress of Hogarth's Rake—from his first appearance in London to his final phase in Whitefriars and Turnbull Street. It is the story of the decline of the Elizabethan gentry, told by a man who is well aware of both its comic and its tragic implications.

As soon as his father dies, the heir dismisses his old family servants and keeps only what the author calls a monkey and a marmoset—a French page and an Italianate serving-man. He takes up with a professional sharper, who dresses like an upstart tailor and who makes a business of preying on young landlords; at the same time he acquires a mistress in Whitefriars—a "most delicate drab of three hundred a-year, some unthrifty gentleman's daughter, who had mortgaged his land to scriveners, sure enough from redeeming again; for so much she seemed by her bringing up, though less by her casting down" (VIII, 79). The young man's pleasures are expensive, and he is soon so deeply in debt to a mercer and a merchant that he is obliged to sign away his land. The scene is the apartment of a famous lawyer near the old Temple Garden. The heir's tenants—called from the country for the purpose— are addressed by the lawyer, who ominously repeats the word *fines*. Then suddenly the heir himself enters, looking very much like a baboon in man's apparel.

His head was dressed up in white feathers like a shuttlecock. . . . His doublet was of a strange cut; and to show the fury of his humour, the collar of it rose up so high and sharp as if it would have cut his throat by daylight. His wings, according to the fashion now, was as little and diminutive as a puritan's ruff. . . . His breeches, a wonder to see, were full as deep as the middle of winter, or the roadway between London and Winchester, and so large and wide withal, that I think within a twelvemonth he

might very well put all his lands in them; and then you may imagine
they were big enough, when they would outreach a thousand
acres: moreover, they differed so far from our fashioned hose in
the country, and from his father's old gascoynes, that his back-
part seemed to us like a monster; the roll of the breeches standing
so low, that we conjectured his house of office, sir-reverence, stood
in his hams. All this while his French monkey bore his cloak of
three pounds a-yard, lined clean through with purple velvet, which
did so dazzle our coarse eyes, that we thought we should have been
purblind ever after, what with the prodigal aspect of that and
his glorious rapier and hangers all bost with pillars of gold, fairer
in show than the pillars in Paul's or the tombs at Westminster. . . .

VIII, 68–70

While the lawyer and the creditors confer, the heir ostenta-
tiously smokes—"one time winding the pipe like a horn at
the Pie-corner of his mouth, which must needs make him
look like a sow-gelder, and another time screwing his face
like one of our country players, which must needs make him
look like a fool" (VIII, 72–73). Once the document is prepared, he dashes the pipe into the chimney-corner—for he
never smokes the same pipe twice—signs his name, buckles
on his rapier and hangers, foppishly bows, and passes down
the stairs without so much as a nod for his tenants.

Time passes and Middleton describes another scene—almost the last in the prodigal's career. He is at Poops's Ordinary throwing dice with a half dozen other gallants. He
screams out oaths, he curses the dice, he calls for new ones.
He plays away his girdle and hangers, his rapier and dagger,
even his glorious cloak, and when at last he leaves, quite
stripped of all his finery, he wears the livery-cloak of his
page, so that he seems rather to wait upon his monkey than
his monkey upon him. His ruin is now complete, and he is
compelled to live by preying upon other heirs, as naïve and
as extravagant as he himself was before.

To conclude, within few days' practice he was grown as absolute
in cheating, and as exquisite in pandarism, that he outstripped all
Greene's books *Of the Art of Cony-catching;* and where before
he maintained his drab, he made his drab now maintain him;
proved the only true captain of vaulting-houses, and the valiant
champion against constables and searchers; feeding upon the sin
of White-Friars, Pict-hatch, and Turnboll-street. Nay, there was
no landed novice now but he could melt him away into nothing,
and in one twelvemonth make him hold all his land between his
legs, and yet but straddle easily neither; no wealthy son of the
city but within less than a quarter he could make all his stock not
worth a Jersey stocking: he was all that might be in dissolute vil-
lany, and nothing that should be in his forefathers' honesty.

VIII, 84–85

The story of the heir brilliantly illustrates Middleton's
wit and powers of observation, as well as another quality
rarely found in his work—compassion for the sufferings of
humble people. For the narrator is a ploughman, one of the
tenants on the heir's estate, and while the heir riots, he sweats
and pays fines and gives up his Christmas revelry. In the
story of the soldier, which follows the story of the heir, this
quality is even more apparent. The soldier fights abroad,
loses an arm and a leg, and returns home with only a month's
pay and "a passport to beg in all countries." His compatriots
wonder at him

as if I had been some sea-monster cast ashore, some jesting at my
deformity, whilst others laughed at the jests: one amongst them,
I remember, likened me to a sea-crab, because I went all of one
side; another fellow vied it, and said I looked like a rabbit cut
up and half-eaten, because my wing and leg, as they termed it,
were departed.   VIII, 95

Threatened with the stocks and the whipping-post, he leaves
the city and retires to the suburbs, hobbling out on Sunday
to beg in Moorfields. But here the constable of Finsbury

seizes him and is about to drag him off to prison when the story abruptly ends. In the second edition of the pamphlet (also published in 1604) Middleton adds still another story —perhaps partly autobiographical—in which he describes the indignities suffered by a poor scholar. Here as before he shows himself acutely aware that something is wrong with the world, but, unlike modern authors, he suggests no reforms. At the end of the work he is content to complain that the iron age has succeeded the golden one, and that money, once used to reward poets and scholars, is now locked up in usurers' chests.

In the second of the two pamphlets, *The Black Book,* the tone is lighter, and there is even more gaiety and wit. The subject is no doubt a sordid one—the underworld of Elizabethan London. The characters are bawds, panders, usurers, catchpolls, and highwaymen; the scenes include a brothel, a usurer's dining-room, a gambling hell at Bezle's Ordinary, and the walks of the Royal Exchange. But Middleton never allows his subject to become merely sordid; he sweetens it with his wit, he uses it as a starting point for amusing similes and ingenious verbal twists. The scene at Mistress Silverpin's is quite typical, a scene in which Lucifer, the narrator of the pamphlet, finds his correspondent, Pierce Penniless (who may easily be intended as a portrait of Nashe himself). The filth of the room is appalling, and yet the style is never wittier, positively exploding in showers of brilliant conceits, each more fantastic than the last.

The testern, or shadow over the bed, was made of four ells of cobwebs, and a number of small spinner's-ropes hung down for curtains: the spindle-shank spiders, which show like great lechers with little legs, went stalking over his head as if they had been conning of *Tamburlaine.* To conclude, there was many such sights to be seen, and all under a penny, beside the lamentable prospect of his hose and doublet, which, being of old Kendal-green, fitly re-

sembled a pitched field, upon which trampled many a lusty corporal.
In this unfortunate tiring-house lay poor Pierce upon a pillow
stuffed with horse-meat; the sheets smudged so dirtily, as if they
had been stolen by night out of Saint Pulcher's churchyard when
the sexton had left a grave open, and so laid the dead bodies wool-
ward: the coverlet was made of pieces a' black cloth clapt together,
such as was snatched off the rails in King's-street at the queen's
funeral.   VIII, 25

Such passages as this and indeed *The Black Book* as a whole
represent Middleton in one of his most characteristic moods.
He is a realist, much more so than in the Falso scenes of *The
Phoenix*. He carefully selects the ugliest and least edifying
elements in the society of his time; he creates a world peopled
only by scoundrels of the most outrageous and most unscrupulous sort. And yet he refuses to be disturbed by this world,
or to moralize, or to restrain his laughter. He finds as much
comedy in filth and vice as other writers find in affectation
and folly.

CHAPTER III

Early Comedies

AFTER he had found himself and had thrown off the romantic influence that still appears in *The Family of Love* and *The Phoenix*, Middleton went on to write four comedies —*Your Five Gallants, Michaelmas Term, A Trick to Catch the Old One,* and *A Mad World, My Masters*—all published or at least entered in the Stationers' Register in 1607–8. All describe contemporary London and all portray the scoundrels who inhabit it, but they nevertheless differ a good deal in tone and emphasis. The first two are comparatively serious studies in manners; they aim to expose and anatomize contemporary vices, to show exactly how various villainies are perpetrated, to give intimate pictures of the more scabrous side of Jacobean life. They are obviously related to Middleton's pamphlets, as well as to the earlier pamphlets of Greene. The last two are at once more frivolous and more universal. They touch lightly and ironically on the eternal conflicts between youth and age, between clever and stupid scoundrels. They are a little like *Volpone* and *The Alchemist*, but they can scarcely owe much either to Jonson or to other contemporary masters. They are perhaps Middleton's most brilliant and most characteristic contribution to the comedy of his age.

I

Your Five Gallants can best be described as a reworking of the material in *The Black Book*, as a second, more serious, and more detailed study of the Elizabethan, or rather the Jacobean, underworld. It is an excellent example of Middleton's interest in manners—a play in which everything is subordinated to the single purpose of portraying an aspect of contemporary society.

The characters are not so much human beings as illustrations—illustrations of various underworld tricks and swindles. One of them is a whoremaster who lives by preying on women, another is a thief who picks pockets and robs on the highway, and still another is a pawnbroker who swindles his clients. A complete description of the *dramatis personae* would, in fact, be a fairly complete catalogue of the vices of London. But though they differ a little in the way they make their livings, the characters are in other respects very much alike. They are all moved by greed and lust, and they are all extremely cynical. They realize that they themselves are depraved, but they feel that in their society everyone else is too. "The world's changed," one of them says; "gentlewomen's falls stand upright now; no sin but has a bolster, that it may lie at ease" (I.i.85–87).

Well, what a horrible age do we live in [says another], that a man cannot have a quean to himself! let him but turn his back, the best of her is chipt away like a court loaf, that when a man comes himself, has nothing but bumbast; and these are two simple chippings here. Does my boy pick and I steal to enrich myself, to keep her, to maintain him? why, this is right the sequence of the world. A lord maintains her, she maintains a knight, he maintains a whore, she maintains a captain. So in like manner the pocket keeps my boy, he keeps me, I keep her, she keeps him; it runs like quicksilver from one to another. III.ii.96–107

Individually the characters are not very impressive; together they give a remarkably distinct view, both of human nature, and of the world in which they live.

The scenes and incidents are as carefully chosen as the

characters and contribute quite as much to the general impression. The play opens in a pawnbroker's establishment, where Frippery, the proprietor, reveals the secrets of his business. He never lends more than a third the value of a pawn, and he rarely accepts a pawn from one client without immediately renting it out to another. There are also revelations about the wiles of courtesans and about the "secret twitch" by which the bawd-gallant Primero has won five hundred pounds at cards. In the second act the scene shifts to Primero's establishment, ostensibly a music school, but actually a brothel. Here the inmates gull their clients and are in turn gulled by the irresistible whore-gallant Tailby. The First Courtesan has just begged a chain of pearl from an admirer when Tailby enters:

> *First Courtesan.* Come,
> Where have you spent the time now from my sight?
> I'm jealous of thy action.
> *Tailby.* Push! I did but walk
> A turn or two in the garden.
> *First Courtesan.* What made you there?
> *Tailby.* Nothing but cropt a flower.
> *First Courtesan.* Some woman's honour, I believe.
> *Tailby.* Foh! is this a woman's honour? . . .
> *First Courtesan.* I do account the world but as my spoil,
> To adorn thee:
> My love is artificial to all others,
> But purity to thee. Dost thou want gold?
> Here, take this chain of pearl, supply thyself.   II.i.293–306

He takes it and she leaves.

> *Second Courtesan.* Was this your vow to me?
> *Tailby.* Pox, what's a kiss to be quite rid of her. . . .
> *Second Courtesan.* 'Tis not a kiss I weigh. . . . 'Tis thy love
> that I suspect.
> *Tailby.* My love? why, by this—what shall I swear by?

Second Courtesan. Swear by this jewel; keep thy oath, keep
   that.

Tailby. By this jewel, then, no creature can be perfect
   In my love but thy dear self.   II.i.310–21

She too leaves and Tailby addresses the Novice:

Why, what do you think of me? make I no difference
'Tween seven years' prostitution and seven days?
Why, you're but in the wane of a maid yet.
You wrong my health in thinking I love them:
Do not I know their populous imperfections?
Why, they cannot live till Easter.   II.i.325–30

Later in the second act there is a gambling party at the
Mitre, arranged by the cheating-gallant Goldstone. Here—
with the aid of his man and a pair of false dice—Goldstone
literally strips Tailby to the breeches. Frippery stands beside
the table, ready to accept each garment that is offered in
pawn. Goldstone has already stolen the two great beakers of
the tavern, substituting specially made false beakers in their
places, and before the scene ends he also steals a gilt goblet,
by hiding it and persuading the vintner to give up the search.
In the third act there is a scene in Combe Park, where the
pocket-gallant Pursenet waylays and robs Tailby, here on his
way to keep an assignation in Kingston. Later in the act, in
another scene at the music school, Pursenet's boy is caught
red-handed, his arm in his victim's pocket. But Pursenet lectures him so severely—and at the same time insists so artfully on his good qualities—that the victim has not the heart
to look for a constable.

Believe me, sir, I much wonder at the alteration of this boy,
where he should get this nature: as good a child to see to, and
as virtuous; he has his creed by heart, reads me his chapter duly
every night; he will not miss you one tittle of the nine command-
ments. . . . I fear he skips o'er one, Thou shalt not steal.

                                             III.v.101–7

. . . he's near allied to many men of worship now yet living; a
fine old man to his father; it would kill his heart, i'faith; he'd
away like a chrisom.   III.v.118–21

Bridewell is clearly out of the question for a boy of such
sterling character, and so he escapes, to pick pockets later in
the play.

Realism could scarcely be carried much farther, and indeed
for four acts the play might well pass as a specimen of modern
naturalistic drama. It is episodic—one could begin just as well
with the fourth act as the first; it is deliberately sordid—the
depravity of the characters is unrelieved, even by the author's
wit; and it is just a little dull. But in the fifth act the tone
completely changes, though it is true that Middleton prepares
for the change much earlier in the play. He introduces a
character named Fitsgrave, a kind of Phoenix in private life,
who makes it his business to spy on the five gallants and to
express the author's views about their behavior. When he has
learned their secrets Fitsgrave gets them to expose themselves
allegorically in a masque, and subsequently punishes them.
He sends off the bawd and the pickpocket's boy to be
whipped, and he insists that the remaining gallants marry
Primero's courtesans.

All this is more than a little bewildering after what has
gone before, and it can only indicate a fundamental incon-
sistency in Middleton's thought. He wants to portray, realis-
tically and even cynically, a world peopled only by successful
scoundrels, a world in which every sin has its bolster that it
may lie at ease; and he also wants to portray a well-ordered
world like that of *The Phoenix,* in which scoundrels, no matter how clever they may be, are in the end invariably brought
to justice. But in the play at hand he never succeeds in convincing the reader that the two worlds are one and the same,
and it is doubtful if he even convinces himself. For in his
other comedies he never attempts the same sort of ending,

and in plays like *A Trick to Catch the Old One* and *A Chaste Maid in Cheapside* he avoids anything that looks like punishment or poetic justice.

Your Five Gallants is Middleton's most ambitious—though scarcely his most successful—study in manners; *Michaelmas Term* is, by comparison, severely limited in scope. It has, properly speaking, only one story to tell, that of the fleecing of the heir from the country, though there are several subsidiary episodes involving an upstart toothdrawer's son and a country wench who becomes a successful whore. The story of the heir is very much like the first narrative in *The Ant and the Nightingale*, with one important exception: the central figure is here not the heir himself but the merchant who ruins him—Ephestian Quomodo, a woollen-draper of London. The play is, in fact, primarily concerned with the English middle class.

Quomodo is, like other members of his class in Middleton, a scoundrel and an avowed enemy of the landed gentry. But perhaps the most interesting thing about him is that he is an incorrigible social climber. He wants his daughter to marry a successful man—

he that can make us rich in custom, strong in friends, happy in suits; bring us into all the rooms a' Sundays, from the leads to the cellar; pop us in with venison till we crack again, and send home the rest in an honourable napkin. . . .   II.iii.41–45

He wants his son to adopt a profession, possibly the law, and accordingly he has sent him to Cambridge and the Inns of Court. But what he wants more than anything else and what he needs as a guarantee of respectability is land—a fine old estate in the country. During the summer he goes to Essex, surveys the ground, and singles out the estate of the young heir Easy. He grows lyrical when he tries to describe it; his pleasure is almost voluptuous.

O that sweet, neat, comely, proper, delicate, parcel of land! like a fine gentlewoman i' th' waist, not so great as pretty, pretty; the trees in summer whistling, the silver waters by the banks harmoniously gliding. I should have been a scholar; an excellent place for a student; fit for my son that lately commenced at Cambridge. . . . II.iii.91–97

Throughout the rest of the play he thinks of the estate as already his own. He dreams of riding down to it with a group of his friends and their wives—

some upon pillions, some upon side-saddles, I and little Thomasine i' th' middle, our son and heir, Sim Quomodo, in a peach-colour taffeta jacket, some horse-length, or a long yard before us;— there will be a fine show on's, I can tell you;—where we citizens will laugh and lie down, get all our wives with child against a bank, and get up again. Stay; hah! hast thou that wit, i'faith? 'twill be admirable: to see how the very thought of green fields puts a man into sweet inventions! IV.i.75–84

He even imagines himself standing by and listening surreptitiously while his friends spread stories of his affluence.

Now come my golden days in. Whither is the worshipful master Quomodo and his fair bed-fellow rid forth? To his land in Essex. Whence comes those goodly load[s] of logs? From his land in Essex. Where grows this pleasant fruit, says one citizen's wife in the Row? At master Quomodo's orchard in Essex. O, O, does it so? I thank you for that good news, i'faith. III.iv.13–19

The story develops slowly and each step is carefully explained. In fact, much of it might almost be a dramatic version of a pamphlet by Greene, written to warn young heirs of the hazards they must encounter in London. Quomodo first finds his victim in the Middle Aisle of St. Paul's, where, shortly after his father's death, he is seen chatting with other young sparks and reading the advertisements on the pillars. But Quomodo does not come forward; he merely instructs his "spirits," Shortyard and Falselight, who are to make the preliminary moves. The scene shifts to an ordinary, where gambling is in progress. Shortyard, pretending to be a prosperous gentleman from Kent, scrapes up an acquaintanceship with Easy, lends him money, and encourages him to lose it. He does so and Shortyard suggests that they borrow more money—from Master Quomodo. The scene shifts again—to Quomodo's shop. The woollen-draper would be glad to accommodate an old acquaintance, but unfortunately he is at the moment short of cash; he can only suggest a two-hundred-pound "commodity" of cloth. Shortyard pretends to hesitate but Easy will not let him refuse. Accordingly the cloth is sent out to be sold, and a "bond" for two hundred pounds is prepared in which—for "custom sake"—Easy's name as well as Shortyard's is included. Exactly a month is allowed for payment. But the bond has scarcely been signed when the cloth comes back. The passage to Middleburgh has just been closed; the market is dead; the great merchants are not buying. Hence Shortyard is obliged to sell his commodity to a small merchant down the street—actually Falselight in disguise—for a mere fraction of its value.

The victim having thus been hooked, it is a simple matter to bring him to the net. Shortyard disappears at the end of a month, and Easy is arrested for the bond. To get bail he pledges everything he has—his whole estate, in fact—so confident is he that Shortyard will rescue him. But Shortyard is nowhere to be found, and the estate is forfeited to Quomodo. Thus for a mere trifle—for not much more than the sixty pounds he originally advanced—Quomodo gets a piece of land worth three hundred a year.

In the first four acts the story is as realistic as anything in Jacobean drama, and the characters are entirely consistent. But in the fifth act there is a change, though it is not quite the same as the change at the end of *Your Five Gallants*. Quomodo suddenly becomes foolish and Easy suddenly becomes clever.[1] Quomodo is represented as another Volpone who is so intoxicated with his own success, and so much the victim of *hubris,* that he attempts an entirely pointless deception—he pretends to be dead. He wants—or so he says—to make sure that in his case the heir does not waste what the father has won, and he wants furthermore to see how deeply his family will grieve. But nothing turns out quite as he had expected. His son rejoices, his spirits cheat him, his daughter marries the wrong man, and his wife promptly takes a second husband—no other than the ruined Easy. He has difficulty proving that he is still alive, and he succeeds only after he has been severely reprimanded in court and has given up all claim to Easy's estate. "Thou art thine own affliction," says the Judge, who then banishes Shortyard and Falselight.

Thus Middleton again succeeds in getting his scoundrels into a courtroom, where punishments can be distributed, but only at the price of weakening his most interesting character. It is true that he has an explanation of Quomodo's conduct, one repeatedly suggested in the dialogue. "Wit destroys wit," says Shortyard. "Deceit is her own foe," says another character. "Craft once known," says Quomodo himself,

> Does teach fools wit, leaves the deceiver none.   V.iii.94-95

But the explanation is not worked out nearly so convincingly here as it is in Middleton's other comedies.

Quomodo is of course the center of interest in *Michaelmas Term;* the minor characters are not much more than a casual comment on another aspect of the age—the importance that it attached to money and dress. The toothdrawer's son is so dazzling in his newly acquired finery that his own mother fails to recognize him. He hires her as a bawd; he even dis-

[1] See W. D. Dunkel, *The Dramatic Technique of Thomas Middleton in His Comedies of London Life* (Chicago, 1925), p. 13.

cusses his own career with her and incidentally expresses the author's views of the new gentility.

> *Lethe.* You must take heed how you speak ill of him, I can tell you, now; he's so employed.
>
> *Mother Gruel.* Employed? for what?
>
> *Lethe.* For his 'haviour, wisdom, and other virtues.
>
> *Mother Gruel.* He, virtues? no, 'tis well known his father was too poor a man to bring him up to any virtues; he can scarce write and read.
>
> *Lethe.* He's the better regarded for that amongst courtiers, for that's but a needy quality.
>
> *Mother Gruel.* If it be so, then he'll be great shortly, for he has no good parts about him.   I.i.299–309

The Country Wench is equally dazzling, once the tailor and the tirewoman have finished their work, and in her case her own father mistakes her for a stranger. Hellgill, the pander who brought her to London, thus comments on the change in her appearance:

> *Hellgill.* You talk of an alteration: here's the thing itself. What base birth does not raiment make glorious? and what glorious births do not rags make infamous? Why should not a woman confess what she is now, since the finest are but deluding shadows, begot between tirewomen and tailors? . . . Who would think now this fine sophisticated squall came out of the bosom of a barn, and the loins of a hay-tosser?
>
> *Country Wench.* Out, you saucy, pestiferous pander! I scorn that, i'faith.
>
> *Hellgill.* Excellent! already the true phrase and style of a strumpet. Stay; a little more of the red, and then I take my leave of your cheek for four and twenty hours.   III.i.1–32

This scene—in which the Country Wench tries on her tires and gowns, hires her father as a servant, and accepts the attentions of two gallants before the very eyes of her keeper—

is perhaps the most successful scene in the play not directly concerned with Quomodo.

Your Five Gallants and *Michaelmas Term* are not perhaps among the finest Jacobean comedies, but they are nevertheless remarkably interesting studies of social confusion. They portray an age in which medieval standards have broken down, in which "degree" has been disregarded, in which all sense of social responsibility has been completely lost. They show class struggling against class, individual against individual; they show the sons of toothdrawers rising to affluence and the sons of gentlemen losing their estates. They show that money, land, and women—the only prizes in the social struggle—are quickly gained and quickly lost, that—as one character puts it—they run like quicksilver from one scoundrel to another. It is certainly not a pretty picture, but it is a vivid and impressive one—a picture that will perhaps always have a special interest for students of the past.[2]

II

A Trick to Catch the Old One contains almost as much information about Jacobean society as the two plays just considered, but in this case the information is incidental. The author rarely chooses his characters because they illustrate particular Jacobean swindles; his subject is here not manners but human nature. Quomodo is scarcely to be understood apart from the society in which he lived; Hoard and Lucre are as universal as the fathers in Terence or the miser in Molière.

The picture of human nature is not perhaps essentially different from that in *Your Five Gallants* and *Michaelmas Term*, but it is more consistent and more completely realistic.

---

[2] See Kathleen M. Lynch, *The Social Mode of Restoration Comedy* (New York and London, 1926), pp. 24–28, and L. C. Knights, *Drama & Society in the Age of Jonson* (London, 1937), pp. 263–69.

There are no innocent characters in *A Trick to Catch the Old One*—no Easys who turn on their oppressors, no Fitsgraves who make a business of unmasking villainy, no judges who appear in the last scene to distribute rewards and punishments. The characters are all of a piece—all scoundrels, all hopelessly and irretrievably bad. For the first time in his career Middleton succeeds in creating a completely consistent world which reflects in all its component parts the utter depravity of human nature.

Middleton's attitude toward his world is or seems to be entirely dispassionate. He stands apart from his characters, he refuses to take sides in the dramatic conflict he portrays. It is for this reason perhaps that his critics have often called him an irresponsible if not actually an immoral writer. He "is no more careful of his ethical than of his other probabilities," Arthur Symons complains.[3] His comedies, Schelling says, are void of "any serious moral reprobation." [4] But the fact is that in plays like *A Trick to Catch the Old One* and *A Mad World, My Masters* he is ironic rather than moralistic. He aims to show that sin is blind and that sinners invariably misunderstand the world in which they live, invariably set in motion the forces that bring about their own ruin. The idea is essentially a moral one, even though Middleton works it out without resorting to the crude and obtrusive morality of a Dekker or a Heywood.

It is no doubt easy to find, in Middleton's earlier plays, a good many examples of incidental irony. In *The Phoenix* the title-character catches a thief and carries him before Falso—the thief's master, the very man who encouraged him to go on the road. In *Michaelmas Term* Quomodo reflects complacently on the profound grief of his wife, ignorant of the

---

[3] *Cambridge History of English Literature* (Cambridge, 1932), VI, 63.
[4] F. E. Schelling, *Elizabethan Playwrights* (New York and London, 1925), p. 186.

fact that she has already taken a second husband. But in the other city comedies the irony is not—or not only—incidental; it is part and parcel of the author's thought, the very substance of his point of view. To portray with complete detachment and a profound sense of irony the unedifying struggles between one scoundrel and another—to create, in fact, a kind of ironic farce—this is Middleton's aim in the comic masterpieces now to be considered.[5]

A Trick to Catch the Old One is a particularly good example of sustained irony—a play in which almost every scene and every incident has its ironic point. But it is also a particularly good example of Middleton's skill in construction, for there is no subplot—unless the short scenes devoted to Dampit can be so called—and all the complications of the main plot arise from a simple situation outlined in the first act. The central character is Witgood, a dissolute young man not unlike the heir in *The Ant and the Nightingale*, who has been ruined by lechery and the avarice of his uncle, the citizen-usurer Lucre. To restore his credit, he passes off his Courtesan as a rich widow and circulates the rumor that he is about to marry her. The trick is immediately successful. His creditors, who before have made the city too hot for him, now insist on lending him money. His uncle at once relents, invites him to the house, entertains the Courtesan and showers her with attentions. Witgood is again respectable. The power of money is brilliantly illustrated, and so too is the gullibility of the unscrupulous men who pursue it. Each of them thinks that he is getting more, though as a matter of fact he is only giving away what he has. The reader is sometimes reminded of *Volpone*, and sometimes of *Timon of Athens*, a play in which some authorities have thought that Middleton himself was concerned.

But as the plot develops the similarity to *Volpone* and

[5] See, however, Knights, *Drama & Society in the Age of Jonson*, pp. 256–69. Knights describes Middleton as a Jacobean Mrs. Behn.

Timon disappears. Lucre has an enemy, his fellow-usurer Hoard, whom he once outwitted in dealings with a ruined heir. Lucre is determined that his nephew shall marry the "widow," Hoard is determined that he shall not, and the rest of the play concerns the contest between these two scoundrels, each intent on undoing the other, each actually undoing himself. To make his nephew more acceptable in the widow's eyes, Lucre lends him money, makes him his heir, and returns—without recompense of any kind—his long-since-forfeited estate. But Hoard in the meantime has not been idle, he has determined to marry the widow himself. He reveals to her Witgood's frailties, and makes an appointment to meet her at a tavern, from which they can secretly elope to Cole Harbor. He reaches the tavern a little before her and discovers that no one has yet arrived but Mistress Florence.

Hoard. What is that Florence? a widow?
Drawer. Yes, a Dutch widow.
Hoard. How?
Drawer. That's an English drab, sir: give your worship good morrow. [*Exit*].
Hoard. A merry knave, i'faith! I shall remember a Dutch widow the longest day of my life.   III.iii.14–20

The widow—the other Dutch widow—appears, the elopement takes place, and the measure of Hoard's happiness is at last full. He has his revenge—"Never did man so crush his enemy," he says—and he has a wife not only large in possessions, but spacious in content;

she's rich, she's young, she's fair, she's wise: when I wake, I think of her lands—that revives me; when I go to bed, I dream of her beauty—and that's enough for me: she's worth four hundred a-year in her very smock, if a man knew how to use it.

IV.iv.5–10

But the lands are no doubt the main thing, and he imagines himself riding triumphantly to Staffordshire, much as Quomodo imagined himself riding to Essex.

But the journey will be all, in troth, into the country; to ride to her lands in state and order following; my brother, and other worshipful gentlemen, whose companies I ha' sent down for already, to ride along with us in their goodly decorum beards, their broad velvet cassocks, and chains of gold twice or thrice double; against which time I'll entertain some ten men of mine own into liveries, all of occupations or qualities; I will not keep an idle man about me: the sight of which will so vex my adversary Lucre —for we'll pass by his door of purpose, make a little stand for [the] nonce, and have our horses curvet before the window— certainly he will never endure it, but run up and hang himself presently.   IV.iv.10–23

Later, difficulties appear—Witgood claims a pre-contract with the widow and threatens to go to law—but Hoard is by this time too much elated with his success to worry about trifles. He buys off Witgood by paying his debts and invites all his acquaintances—friend and foe alike—to a triumphant wedding-dinner. Here, however, his shame is finally revealed— his wife is recognized as Witgood's mistress—and he now has even better reason to remember what a Dutch widow is. "So, so, all friends!" he says,

> So, so, all friends! the wedding-dinner cools:
> Who seem most crafty prove ofttimes most fools.   V.ii.206–7

I have mentioned the construction—always one of Middleton's strongest points—and in this case perhaps it deserves closer examination. The expository material in the first act is lucidly and entertainingly presented. Witgood is introduced, then the Courtesan, then their accomplice, the Host; at the same time the details of Witgood's trick are clearly explained. The following scenes introduce Lucre and Hoard —who give an amusing display of verbal spitting—and the minor character of Dampit. In the second act the results of the trick begin to appear. Lucre entertains the Courtesan and encourages his nephew to marry her; Hoard determines to marry her himself. In the third act Witgood's success is assured. His creditors fawn on him and Hoard elopes with the Courtesan—just in the nick of time. In the fourth act Witgood gets what he wants from both of the adversaries, and the Courtesan gets what she wants—marriage. The fifth act is devoted to the wedding-dinner at which the Courtesan's identity is finally disclosed. There are only two weaknesses— the scene of the pre-contract, which looks like an afterthought, and the character of Dampit, who gets so little attention that he scarcely deserves a place in the play at all. Otherwise an almost perfect unity is achieved. It is not, of course, the massive architectural unity achieved by Jonson in such a play as *The Alchemist*, where many characters of distinctly different types are welded into the framework of a single action, but in its own way and on its own scale it is almost equally satisfying.

A Mad World, My Masters is more fantastic than *A Trick*, and even more hilarious. The title is in this case particularly happy; the play creates a world of preposterous tricks, uproarious surprises, sudden and ironic changes of fortune. Follywit, the principal character in the main plot, is Witgood all over again. "I was as well given till I fell to be wicked," he says of himself—he of course paraphrases Falstaff—

my grandsire had hope of me: I went all in black; swore but a' Sundays; never came home drunk but upon fasting-nights to cleanse my stomach. 'Slid, now I'm quite altered! blown into light colours; let out oaths by th' minute; sit up late till it be early; drink drunk till I am sober; sink down dead in a tavern, and rise in a tobacco-shop! here's a transformation! I was wont yet to pity the simple, and leave 'em some money! 'slid, now I gull 'em without conscience! I go without order, swear without number, gull without mercy, and drink without measure. I.i.13–24

He has learned, in short, to live by his wits, and since his grandfather has money, what more natural than that he too

should be gulled along with the rest? For the grandfather
has an obvious weakness suggested by his name, Sir Bounteous Progress. He is extremely hospitable; he loves to entertain; he takes great delight in displaying his house with its
great turret, his fish-ponds, his park, his cloth-of-gold chamber, and his organ, double-gilt. Even the beds in his mansion
have cambric sheets and cloth-of-tissue canopies.

. . . the curtains, indeed, were wrought in Venice, with the story
of the Prodigal Child in silk and gold; only the swine are left
out . . . for spoiling the curtains.   II.ii.5–8

Into this luxurious establishment Follywit enters disguised
as Lord Owemuch, with his lewd companions as a retinue. He
accepts the most lavish entertainment from Sir Bounteous and
then in the night rises and robs him. He ties him up and ties
himself up as well, for he is determined to leave as he came—
like a lord. "I'll not have the jest spoiled," he says, "that's
certain, though it hazard a windpipe." In the morning Sir
Bounteous is profuse in his apologies and insists on making
good the handsome sum that Lord Owemuch has lost. "Can
you not guess what [the robbers] should be?" asks Follywit.

> *Sir Bounteous.* Faith, Lincolnshire men, my lord.
> *Follywit.* How? fie, fie, believe it not, sir; these lie not far off,
>   I warrant you.
> *Sir Bounteous.* Think you so, my lord?
> *Follywit.* I'll be burnt and they do; some that use to your
>   house, sir, and are familiar with all the conveyances.
>   II.vii.46–53

The robbery is so profitable and the jest is so good that Follywit tries again, this time disguised as his grandfather's Courtesan. He kisses the old man at the bottom of the stairs,
ascends to an upper chamber, and rifles a casket of the jewelry
it contains. The kiss was perhaps a mistake, and Sir Bounteous
later comments on it. "Methought her breath had much ado
to be sweet," he says; "like a thing compounded, methought,

of wine, beer, and tobacco; I smelt much pudding in't."
But his suspicions are not really aroused, even when he discovers the robbery.

Follywit is so completely successful that he is inclined to regard himself as an instrument of retribution:

I am sure my grandsire ne'er got his money worse in his life than I got it from him. If ever he did cozen the simple, why, I was born to revenge their quarrel; if ever oppress the widow, I, a fatherless child, have done as much for him. And so 'tis through the world, either in jest or earnest. Let the usurer look for't; for craft recoils in the end, like an overcharged musket, and maims the very hand that puts fire to't. III.iii.5–13

It does indeed—his own craft is about to recoil upon him, his own wit to destroy itself. He meets his grandfather's Courtesan and falls in love with her at first sight, completely taken in by her skillfully feigned modesty. " 'Sfoot, this is strange!" he says,

> I've seldom seen a wench
> Stand upon stricter points: life, she will not
> Endure to be courted! does she e'er think to prosper?
> IV.v.4–6

But she does endure it—her Mother insists—and with all her diffidence she promptly accepts him as a husband. The irony of the scene is delicious.

Follywit. Fear not. Come,
    Erect thy happy graces in thy look;
    I am no curious wooer, but, in faith,
    I love thee honourably. . . .
                    I've a grandsire
    Will make me lord of thousands at his death.
Mother. I know your grandsire well; she knows him better. . . .
Follywit. . . . I warrant you he'll drop away at fall a' th' leaf;
    If e'er he reach to All Hollantide, I'll be hang'd.
Mother. O yes, son, he's a lusty old gentleman.

Follywit. Ah, pox, he's given to women! keeps a quean at this
   present.
Mother. Fie!
Follywit. Do not tell my wife on't.
Mother. That were needless, i'faith.   IV.v.95–129

More than ever pleased with himself, Follywit decides to
play still another trick on Sir Bounteous. He appears before
him as the chief actor in a company of strollers, borrows from
him a watch, a jewel, and a chain—to be used, he says, as
properties in the play—and speaks a prologue while his companions escape. But the companions immediately reappear—
conducted by the constable, who has taken them up on suspi-
cion—and Follywit has to pretend that the constable is a
character in the play. The stratagem is perhaps his masterpiece—he binds and gags the constable before his grandfather's very eyes. But when, a moment later, he appears in
his own dress, the alarm on the watch goes off in his pocket
and everything is revealed. He excuses himself as best he .
can and insists that he has not only reformed but taken a
wife—both a gentlewoman and a virgin.

   Sir Bounteous. Stop there, stop there: would I might see her!
   Follywit. You have your wish; she's here.
   Sir Bounteous. Ah, ha, ha, ha! this makes amends for all.
   Follywit. How now?
   Mawworm. Captain, do you hear? is she your wife in ear-
      nest? . . .
   Follywit. Is't come about? tricks are repaid, I see.
   Sir Bounteous. The best is, sirrah, you pledge none but me;
      And since I drink the top, take her—and, hark,
      I spice the bottom with a thousand mark.   V.ii.275–91

The reversal is complete, the wit is himself outwitted.
   In the underplot the irony is a little less amusing perhaps
but even more obvious. Harebrain is so jealous of his wife
that he allows her only one companion—a "pure virgin" who

specializes in "good counsel." The virgin is the Courtesan of Sir Bounteous, and the counsel is if anything too good, for Mistress Harebrain promptly takes a lover. She meets him at the Courtesan's house while her husband waits at the door, well satisfied with the way she is spending her time. But the lover, whose name is Penitent Brothel, has a strong sense of sin which ultimately overwhelms him. He confronts his mistress, lectures her on the evils of adultery, and persuades her to vow eternal fidelity to her husband. She does so, on her knees, and just at this moment the husband enters. Again he congratulates himself. "Two dear rare gems this hour presents me with,/" he says, "A wife that's modest and a friend that's right." The mechanism of the lover's conversion—the succubus that appears before him in the shape of Mistress Harebrain—is a little disconcerting perhaps, but scarcely out of place in this sort of comedy.

To follow a summary of a play like *A Mad World* is perhaps to get some idea of the liveliness of Middleton's plots. His comedy is seldom static; his characters are seldom satisfied with talk. The scoundrels clash, plot and counterplot, cudgel their brains devising stratagems, each more outrageous than the last, and if one of the scoundrels thinks he has achieved a complete victory, it always turns out that he has not. If a usurer succeeds in marrying a widow and winning a rich estate, he must later discover that the widow is a whore —his enemy's whore, in fact. If an heir has his grandfather's watch in his pocket and seems certain to escape, the alarm on the watch must go off and the heir himself must be caught. The action must never pause; there must always be excitement, bustle, and surprise.

But it is much more difficult to get from a summary an idea of the liveliness of Middleton's dialogue, which contributes quite as much as the action to the general hilarity. For Middleton is a genuinely witty writer, though less studied and less consistently successful than the best Restoration dramatists. He resorts to whatever form of wit occurs to him at the moment; he uses the pun, the epigram, and the *double-entendre*. He is particularly fond of the last, which he exploits more unscrupulously and more amusingly than any of his contemporaries. But he is perhaps seen at his best in wit that is rooted in his irony—in quite unpretentious lines, meaningless apart from their context, which illuminate the relations of the characters and underscore the author's point of view. An example is the Mother's remark to Follywit in the passage quoted above: "I know your grandsire well; she knows him better." It is a line charged with irony, one that reveals even better than the action itself the uproarious comedy of Follywit's deception.

If it were not for Middleton's wit, if it were not for his persistent light-heartedness, plays like *A Trick* and *A Mad World* would be almost intolerable. They would be disquieting studies of the repulsive and the abnormal, dark probings into the ulcerous side of human nature. They would be more disquieting—because they are more prosaic—than the darkest pages of *The Phoenix*, more disquieting even than *The Revenger's Tragedy* itself. But as it is, they are not only tolerable but hilarious. The vices of the characters are so entertaining that they scarcely seem to be vices; the moral law operates so pleasantly that it scarcely seems to be a moral law at all. Distinguished critics can even complain that Middleton has no morality, that he gives sympathetic portraits of characters like Follywit, and that he lets them off without adequate punishment. But surely this is an extreme view. Middleton is not indeed bitter in these plays; he laughs at scoundrels who insist on undoing themselves, laughs even at the end of their careers when they find themselves married to whores. But laughter and sympathy are scarcely the same thing, and the comedy of a writer who refuses to be disturbed by human depravity is not necessarily irresponsible.

In an earlier passage I have suggested that the city comedies just described are more completely realistic than *Your Five Gallants* and *Michaelmas Term*—more realistic in the sense that they contain more hopelessly depraved characters. But in another sense, they can scarcely be called realistic at all. Their incidents are often improbable, their picture of contemporary life is often anything but "photographic." [6] They begin no doubt in London, but they soon drift off into a fantastic world in which the strangest things happen—in which sharpers disguised as lords are entertained by their grandfathers, and succubi disguised as mistresses discourage adulterous lovers. It is no doubt a question of emphasis, but such plays are certainly closer to *The Silent Woman* than to *Bartholomew Fair*, closer to the work of Gilbert than to the work of Gorki. They are, in short, primarily farces, and they perhaps deserve to be ranked with the most distinguished plays of their type in the English language—plays that, despite the frivolity of their mood and the improbability of their action, are quite as amusing as many more pretentious masterpieces.

[6] T. S. Eliot, *Selected Essays, 1917–1932* (New York, 1932), p. 147, and Schelling, *Elizabethan Playwrights*, pp. 186–87.

CHAPTER IV

The Revenger's Tragedy

ONCE attributed to Tourneur, *The Revenger's Tragedy* has so much in common with Middleton's early work that it must be regarded as almost certainly his. It is like *The Phoenix* in its bitterness, like *A Mad World* and *A Trick* in its irony, like *Your Five Gallants* in its concern with an aspect of contemporary society, in this case the court. But it is more imaginative than any of them, more completely divorced from manners, English or Italian, and more completely concerned with the dark and fetid atmosphere of the world that it portrays.

In the first scene the hero watches with a skull in his hand while the chief figures of the court pass across the stage in the torchlight, like a procession of the Seven Deadly Sins. He describes them, apostrophizes the skull, and calls on vengeance, "murders Quit-rent," to keep her "day, houre, minute." Thus the tone is set, thus the subjects of sin and death are announced; the nightmare is ready to begin. And what a nightmare it is! what a hideous picture of vice and corruption! The characters are not so much human beings as automata driven by devils, dancing in wild gyrations of treachery and lust. They plot and kill, rape and engender. They harry their victims with panders; they creep unbraced through dark passages, their valiant bawds at their backs; they steal out their swords during masques, intent on wholesale slaughter. They recognize no law, either human or divine, and yet in the end an inexorable law overtakes them. It strikes with the thunder from on high, it glares from the comets that balefully shake their beards.

The characters recognize no law, they are the victims of their own irresponsible passions; but as one gets into the play one realizes that they are quite as clearly the victims of their own stupidity. For they are not nearly so clever as they think they are. They are constantly making the most glaring mistakes, inviting disaster and rushing on destruction with open arms. It is for this reason, of course, that their careers are so profoundly ironical and so much like the careers of Lucre and Hoard in Middleton's comedy. They are further illustrations of a favorite theme of Middleton's, that of the biter bit.[1]

The hero—the famous Vindice—stands a little apart from the others. He is not so much a sinner himself, though he ultimately becomes one, as a man who loathes sinners, and not so much a man as a volcano. His function in the play is, first of all, to erupt—to deliver, like Prince Phoenix, appropriately sulphurous denunciations—and the action is arranged so that he is in a state of eruption much of the time. Drama is used to provide opportunities for rhetoric and satire, lurid outbursts in which the views of the author are presumably expressed. Thus, when Vindice puts on a disguise, he apostrophizes Impudence ("Thou Goddesse of the pallace, Mistris of Mistresses/ To whom the costly-perfumd people pray"); when he undertakes to do some pimping, he talks about "Dutch lust! fulsome lust!/ Druncken procreation"; when he is asked what reward he wants for pimping successfully accomplished, he specifies "the fees behind the *Arras;* and all the farthingales that fal plumpe about twelue a clock

---

[1] M. C. Bradbrook, *Themes and Conventions of Elizabethan Tragedy* (Cambridge, 1935), p. 165: "The narrative illustrates with ingenious variety in how many ways a villain may be hoist with his own petard."

at night vpon the Rushes"; and when he is doing nothing in
particular except watching people go by, he apostrophizes
the time of day—nighttime, of course.

> Now tis full sea a bed ouer the world;
> Theres iugling of all sides; some that were Maides
> E'en at Sun set a.e now perhaps ith Toale-booke;
> This woman in immodest thin apparell
> Lets in her friend by water, here a Dame
> Cunning, nayles lether-hindges to a dore,
> To auoide proclamation.
> Now Cuckolds are a quoyning, apace, apace, apace, apace.
> And carefull sisters spinne that thread ith night,
> That does maintaine them and their bawdes ith daie!
>
> II.ii.152–61

The subject is usually sex, preferably in its more sensational
forms, but in the third act, where the skull reappears, the
emphasis is a little different. Vindice is for the time being
another Hamlet brooding in the graveyard, dwelling on the
vanity of human wishes and the imminence of death.

> And now me thinkes I cold e'en chide my selfe,
> For doating on her beauty, tho her death
> Shall be reuengd after no common action;
> Do's the Silke-worme expend her yellow labours
> For thee? for thee dos she vndoe herselfe?
> Are Lord-ships sold to maintaine Lady-ships
> For the poore benefit of a bewitching minute?
>
> Dos euery proud and selfe-affecting Dame
> Camphire her face for this? and grieue her Maker
> In sinfull baths of milke,—when many an infant starues,
> For her superfluous out-side, all for this? . . .
> Here might a scornefull and ambitious woman
> Looke through and through her selfe,—see Ladies, with false
> formes
> You deceiue men, but cannot deceiue wormes.
>
> III.v.72–78, 87–101

Vindice has, however, another function in the play quite as important as his function as commentator. He is the instrument of the author's irony when such an instrument is needed, the means by which the depravity of the other characters is disclosed and punished. In this respect, too, he is similar to Prince Phoenix, for he is constantly turning up where he is least expected, usually in disguise, and constantly taking advantage of error and weakness. The situation recurs so frequently that it might easily become monotonous in the hands of a less accomplished writer.

In the first two acts the hero's principal victim is the Duke's eldest son, Lussurioso, one of the ugliest monsters in the play and one of the most lecherous. "His heate is such," Vindice says,

> Were there as many Concubines as Ladies
> He would not be contaynd, he must flie out:
> I wonder how ill featurde, vilde proportiond
> That one should be: if she were made for woman,
> Whom at the Insurrection of his lust
> He would refuse for once.

I.i.90–96

At the moment he is interested in debauching the virtuous Castiza, and since he has a sense of irony, he asks one of Castiza's brothers to provide him with a suitable pander. But since the brother also has a sense of irony, he produces another brother, Vindice in fact, who here pretends to be a notable pander and an old hand with virgins. Lussurioso is so deeply impressed that he at once betrays himself. He charges a brother with a sister's ruin, and indeed boasts of his wit at precisely the moment he is being outwitted.

Lussurioso. That was her brother
  That did prefer thee to vs. . . .
  We may laugh at that simple age within him.
Vindice. Ha, ha, ha.

Lussurioso. Himselfe being made the subtill instrument,
 To winde vp a good fellow.
Vindice. That's I my Lord.
Lussurioso. That's thou.
 To entice and worke his sister.
Vindice. A pure nouice!
Lussurioso. T'was finely manag'd.   I.iii.148–63

The episode is very much like the one in *The Phoenix* in which Proditor charges a son with his father's murder.

Vindice moves relentlessly forward and by the third act he has so well disposed of Lussurioso that he is ready to turn his attention to the Duke. The scene is a central one in that it directly determines the catastrophe and in that it comes closer perhaps than any other scene to epitomizing what is most characteristic in Middleton's strange drama. The Duke is described as an even more fantastic example of license than his son—a "parcht and iuicelesse luxur" whose hollow bones are stuffed "with dambd desires." But since his intelligence is by no means commensurate with his lust, and since he is guided by the same perverse instinct as his son, he turns to his worst enemy for help, the same enemy in fact. He too hires Vindice as a pander. A lady is to be provided

> In some fit place vaylde from the eyes ath Court,
> Some darkned blushlesse Angle, that is guilty
> Of his fore-fathers lusts, and great-folkes riots. III.v.15–17

Vindice is nothing if not diabolical. He arranges the assignation in an "vn-sunned lodge" where the Duchess and her incestuou. lover meet, and instead of a lady he provides a skull "drest up in Tires"—the skull of his own mistress, whom the Duke poisoned nine years before when she rejected his advances. And since Vindice's conception of punishment is almost exactly that of Gilbert's Mikado, he anoints the teeth of the skull with poison. "Looke you brother," he says to Hippolito,

I haue not fashiond this onely—for show
And vselesse property; no, it shall beare a part
E'en in it owne Reuenge. This very skull,
Whose Mistris the Duke poysoned, with this drug
The mortall curse of the earth, shall be reuengd
In the like straine, and kisse his lippes to death.   III.v.102–8

In the earlier scenes of the play Vindice is associated with the emotions of anger when he is concerned with his own wrongs and moral indignation when he is concerned with the court generally. But in the scene before us his anger seems quite drained from him and he feels nothing but elation, so violent that he himself is repeatedly tempted to describe it. "I'me in a throng of happy Apprehensions," he exclaims.

O sweete, delectable, rare, happy, rauishing.
O tis able to make a man spring vp, & knock his for-head
Against yon siluar seeling.

He is elated because his long-awaited vengeance is finally at hand and, furthermore, because he is showing so much ingenuity in working it out—what Hippolito calls so much "quaintresse" in his "malice." When the Duke approaches and asks about the lady, Vindice's elation takes the form of quite inhuman, quite ghoulish jocularity, not very different from that displayed by the Machiavellians in earlier tragedy.

Faith my Lord a Country Lady, a little bashfull at first as most of them are, but after the first kisse my Lord the worst is past with them; your grace knowes now what you haue to doo; sha's some-what a graue looke with her—but—   III.v.140–43

The Duke kisses the skull and smears his face with the poison. The brothers trample on him, stab him, and force him to watch as his Duchess and his bastard reveal their lust, for this too plays a part in the quaintness. Meanwhile Vindice's jocularity becomes positively hysterical.

Duke. My teeth are eaten out.
Vindice. Hadst any left?

Hippolito. I thinke but few.
Vindice. Then those that did eate are eaten.
Duke. O my tongue.
Vindice. Your tongue? twill teach you to kisse closer,
  Not like a Flobbering *Dutchman.*   III.v.169–75

When the Duke, unable to endure his torment any longer, mutters, "I cannot brooke—" and dies, Vindice delivers the most outrageously jocular of all his comments. "The Brooke," he says, "is turnd to bloud."   .

In this scene and the scenes that follow it Vindice is somewhat less like Prince Phoenix and somewhat more like the characters in Middleton's comedies, specifically Follywit in *A Mad World, My Masters.* For Vindice is now shown to be another example of the clever man who is blinded by his own cleverness, the self-satisfied hero who turns out to be anything but a hero in the end. The plays in which he and Follywit appear are in fact companion pieces and quite obviously—if the reader takes the trouble to compare them—the work of the same man. In *A Mad World* Follywit's self-satisfaction becomes evident in the third act when he boasts about his virtuosity and describes himself as an instrument of retribution. "Peace," he exclaims as he suddenly sees how he can display his virtuosity again,

> Peace, 'tis mine own, i'faith; I ha't! . .
> Thanks, thanks to any spirit
> That mingled it 'mongst my inventions!   III.iii.68–71

and he goes on to assure his companions that there will be no delay.

> And thou shalt see't quickly, i'faith: nay, 'tis in grain; I warrant it hold colour.   III.iii.81–82

The passage is pretty clearly a transitional one, designed to prepare the reader for Follywit's deception. In the third and fourth acts of *The Revenger's Tragedy* Vindice makes similar boasts about *his* virtuosity and thinks of *himself* as an instrument of retribution. Then suddenly he too cries out as a new and particularly ingenious idea occurs to him:

> But I haue found it.
> Twill hold, tis sure, thankes, thankes to any spirit,
> That mingled it mongst my inuentions,   IV.ii.226–28

and he goes on to reassure his brother.

> Nay doubt not tis in graine, I warrant it hold collour.
> IV.ii.255

Thus in his case the transition is made; thus the reader is prepared for the final reversal, in which Vindice, ostensibly the hero of the play, suddenly becomes his own victim.

Vindice's new idea is indeed quite wonderfully ingenious and he certainly has some reason to be pleased with himself. He reveals the Duke's murder without in any way implicating himself—he stabs the dead body in the presence of Lussurioso, pretending all the while that the Duke is not dead and is indeed someone else, the murderer himself in fact, lying in a drunken stupor. As the preposterous performance proceeds, Vindice amuses himself and his brother with characteristically ghoulish comments.

> *Vindice.* Shall we kill him now hees drunke?
> *Lussurioso.* I best of all.
> *Vindice.* Why then hee will nere liue to be sober?
> *Lussurioso.* No matter, let him reele to hell.
> *Vindice.* But being so full of liquor, I feare hee will put out all the fire.
> *Lussurioso.* Thou art a mad beast.
> *Vindice.* And leaue none to warme your Lordships Gols withall; For he that dyes drunke, falls into hell fire like a Bucket a water, qush, qush.   V.i.49–57

Subsequently he congratulates himself again,

> Thus much by wit a deepe Reuenger can:
> When murders knowne, to be the cleerest man.

> We're fordest off, and with as bould an eye,
> Suruay his body as the standers by,   V.i.96–99

and when the wrong man is sent off to execution he and
Hippolito congratulate each other.

> *Hippolito.* Brother how happy is our vengeance.
> *Vindice.* Why it hits, past the apprehension of indifferent wits.
>   V.i.143–44

Such passages—since self-satisfied characters obviously have
very little to look forward to in Middleton—complete the
preparation for the catastrophe, soon announced by a minor
and indeed nameless character, a mere Nobleman. "No
doubt," he says,

>   but time
> Wil make the murderer bring forth him-selfe.   V.i.168–69

Vindice scoffs but the remark is highly significant nevertheless
—one of the keys to his role in the play in fact. For this is
not, as the reader is at first inclined to suppose, a revenge
tragedy, but something quite different, a revenger's tragedy.
It is the story of a man who commits a perfect crime and then
becomes so pleased with his performance that he gives himself away. He is ruined by his cleverness or his stupidity, de-
pending on one's point of view—in any case, by his inability
to keep his mouth shut at the right time.

Vindice commits another crime, the murder of Lussurioso,
and again the wrong man is sent off to execution. Vindice is
by this time positively bursting with self-satisfaction, and so,
when the new duke wants to know how the old duke was
killed, he cannot help telling him how it was done. Quite
suddenly, as in farces, the revenger himself is hustled off to
the block, but not before he has had time to generalize about
what has happened. "When murders shut deeds closse," he
says,

>   this curse does seale 'em,
> If none disclose 'em they them selues reueale 'em!

This murder might haue slept in tonglesse brasse,
But for our selues, and the world dyed an asse.   V.iii.155–58

He goes on to emphasize the comic aspect of his catastrophe
by recalling good-naturedly—but somewhat inaccurately, as
it happens, for he is wrong about the speaker—the remark
of the Nobleman.

Now I remember too, here was *Piato*
Brought forth a knauish sentance once—no doubt (said he)
but time
Will make the murderer bring forth himselfe.   V.iii.159–61

In any case, the wheel has come full circle; the tragedy of
the revenger has been accomplished.[2]

I follow Middleton in using the word *tragedy*, and yet
I cannot help thinking that the play is really a kind of melodramatic farce. The characters lack the stature and the in-
dividuality associated with genuine tragic action. They are all,
as I have said, very much like automata, quite without interest in themselves, designed merely to follow certain fixed
and formal patterns prescribed by the author and to illustrate
his favorite ideas. Even Vindice is incompletely individualized.
The drama in which he plays a part is always highly sim-
plified and stylized, always wonderfully neat and effective,
but perhaps just for this reason somewhat lacking in humanity.
Despite its sombre beginning and its many lurid episodes,
it is obviously related to comedy and, I might add, to ballet.
The patterns in which the characters move are dancelike, and
in the final scene the *corps de ballet* actually puts in an appearance. A blazing star, a particularly dreadful one, has just
been seen in the heavens, when masquers begin weaving back
and forth across the stage—first a masque of revengers, who
inevitably stab a few spectators as they finish, and then a
masque of intended murderers, who, not finding any victims

[2] A somewhat different view of the conclusion is expressed in Robert Orn-
stein, "The Ethical Design of *The Revenger's Tragedy*," ELH, XXI
(June, 1954), 81–93.

left, turn their swords upon each other. The dialogue is
for the time being pretty much limited to the groans of the
dying and peals of thunder, which—repeatedly invoked by
the hero throughout the play—now finally sounds again.

In my summary I have overemphasized the part played by
the hero and thus perhaps misrepresented the construction
of the play, which is a little like that in *Your Five Gallants.*
The attention of the reader is divided among half-a-dozen
groups of figures, all exemplifying somewhat similar vices
and all about equally important. At times there may be some
confusion, as the critics have occasionally complained, but
there are certainly compensating advantages. The author is
able to give a broad view of court life and to diversify it with
episodes, some—like the wonderful episode of Gratiana in the
fourth act—not strictly essential. At the same time he is able
to illustrate repeatedly his doctrine of retribution. The cumu-
lative effect is very impressive.

The style is appropriately harsh and angular. Middleton
likes crude and vigorous brush strokes—the word play and
antithesis exemplified in the speeches of Vindice—but what
he likes best of all is rhyme. He uses it to emphasize his
rhetoric—to mark off his aphorisms and give satirical point
to his dialogue—and since he is always in a hurry he is inclined to be satisfied with almost any rhyme that comes to
hand. Inverting the normal word order or otherwise doing
violence to idiom, disregarding the niceties of meter or rely-
ing on inferior imagery—these things seem to mean nothing
to him so long as the rhyme-words come. Examples are
hazardous since language has changed a good deal in the
last three hundred years, but I venture to think that the
following couplets were not entirely happy even at the time
they were written.

> Let her requite it now, tho it be but some;
> You brought her forth, she may well bring you home.

> II.i.114–15

For Lawiers, Merchants, some diuines and all,
Count beneficiall perjury a sin small.   II.ii.112–13

In thine owne shape now, ile prefer thee to him:
How strangely does himselfe worke to vndo him.

IV.i.70–71

Faith Brother he himselfe showes the way.
Now the Duke is dead, the realme is clad in claye.

IV.ii.14–15

In any case, the couplets jingle somewhat naïvely and in short passages the effect is not altogether pleasing. When, however, the play is read act by act or as a whole at a single sitting, the faults seem insignificant and what stands out is Middleton's wonderful force and terseness. Even as he hurries forward he is able to toss off images—often confined to a single word—that can only be described as inevitable and imaginative in the very highest degree. Liquor is "wet damnation," the labors of the silkworm are "yellow," temptation is a "black serpent" that is wound about the victim and must afterwards be untwisted. When Gratiana kneels and weeps, the hero thus addresses his weapon:

Nay and you draw teares once, go you to bed,
Wet will make yron blush and change to red:
Brother it raines, twill spoile your dagger, house it.

IV.iv.51–53

Bed, blush, raines, house—metaphor succeeds metaphor characteristically and indeed inevitably. This is great dramatic verse, comparable in its concentration, if not in its splendor, to the verse in *Volpone* and *The White Devil*. It is one of the monumental achievements of the Jacobean stage.

CHAPTER V

Later Comedies

BETWEEN about 1608 and 1627 Middleton wrote, or helped to write, at least fourteen plays—six comedies, five tragicomedies, and four tragedies. Of the three groups the comedies are by far the least interesting. An early one, *A Chaste Maid in Cheapside,* is indeed distinguished, but the later comedies are decidedly inferior to Middleton's best work—less amusing, less original in their material, and less consistent in their point of view. It is possible that Middleton tired of comic writing as he grew older and that he did it, when he had to, rather perfunctorily. But it is more likely that he was misled by the example of such fashionable writers as Beaumont and Fletcher and that he tried to give his audience the kind of comedy that, at the moment, it liked best. If this was his purpose, he succeeded—he wrote a good many smart comic scenes during the last ten years of his career—but he succeeded only at the expense of betraying his own genius and suppressing his most distinctive qualities.

I

The celebrated comedy of *The Roaring Girl,* so highly praised by T. S. Eliot, is not a good example of Middleton's declining power, simply because it is not really his work at all.[1] For in this play he had a collaborator, Thomas Dekker, and during the greater part of it he was apparently content

[1] T. S. Eliot, *Selected Essays, 1917–1932* (New York, 1932), p. 147.

to fill in the outlines of Dekker's plan. He contributed indeed to the sentimental portrait of Moll Cutpurse, the principal character. Of the seven scenes in which she appears four seem to be largely his and another one may well be his too, but the point of view is always Dekker's. Who but Dekker would have thought of portraying a female eccentric in breeches who shows her good nature by refusing to steal a watch and chain? Yet the incident occurs in one of the scenes apparently written by Middleton. The underplot, in which two citizens' wives encourage but later expose their lovers, seems also to be Dekker's invention. But in these scenes Middleton's share is not quite so humble; at the beginning of the second act at least he succeeds in marking the characters with his cynicism and the dialogue with his wit. Here, for example, is an entirely characteristic passage about three young sparks who throw off epigrams and *doubles-entendres* as they approach the shop of Mistress Gallipot:

> *Goshawk.* Is that she?
> *Laxton.* Peace.
> *Greenwit.* She that minces tobacco?
> *Laxton.* Ay; she's a gentlewoman born, I can tell you, though it be her hard fortune now to shred Indian pot-herbs.
> *Goshawk.* O sir, 'tis many a good woman's fortune, when her husband turns bankrout, to begin with pipes and set up again.
> *Laxton.* And, indeed, the raising of the woman is the lifting up of the man's head at all times; if one flourish, t'other will bud as fast, I warrant ye.
> *Goshawk.* Come, thou'rt familiarly acquainted there, I grope that. II.i.6–19

Dekker is seldom so sharp, but the final episode of the underplot is clearly marked as Dekker's by its genial and whimsical style.

The praise that Eliot has lavished on *The Roaring Girl* might better have been saved for *A Chaste Maid in Cheap-*

side, which is indeed a great play and in many respects an
epitome of all the comic work that Middleton had so far
done. Like *Your Five Gallants* and *Michaelmas Term,* it
is concerned—or at least partly concerned—with contemporary
manners; but it is more complex in its structure, more massive
in its effect than the earlier plays, and it gives a broader
picture of Jacobean life. The *dramatis personae* is large:
citizens and knights, students and fortune-hunters, barren
men and fruitful men, wittols and whores crowd the pages.
Each is distinctly realized and each helps to illuminate the
contemporary scene. As a study in manners, in fact, the play
is unsurpassed in Jacobean drama, except perhaps by *The
Alchemist* and *Bartholomew Fair.* Many illustrations might
be given but two at least are inevitable—the scene of the
promoters and the scene of the christening.

Promoters were official spies who haunted the streets during
Lent, looking for meat and confiscating whatever they found.
The promoters of the play are thus described by another
character:

> Ha, how now? what are these that stand so close
> At the street-corner, pricking up their ears
> And snuffing up their noses, like rich men's dogs
> When the first course goes in? By the mass, promoters;
> 'Tis so, I hold my life; and planted there
> T' arrest the dead corps of poor calves and sheep,
> Like ravenous creditors, that will not suffer
> The bodies of their poor departed debtors
> To go to th' grave, but e'en in death to vex
> And stay the corps with bills of Middlesex.
> This Lent will fat the whoresons up with sweetbreads,
> And lard their whores with lamb-stones: what their golls
> Can clutch goes presently to their Molls and Dolls:
> The bawds will be so fat with what they earn,
> Their chins will hang like udders by Easter-eve,
> And, being stroak'd, will give the milk of witches.

> II.ii.54–69

A man enters with a basket of meat concealed under his cloak, and the promoters seize the meat.

> *Man.* Now, a pox choke you!
>   You've cozen'd me and five of my wife's kindred
>   Of a good dinner; we must make it up now
>   With herrings and milk-pottage.
> *First Promoter.* 'Tis all veal.
> *Second Promoter.* All veal?
>   Pox, the worse luck! I promised faithfully
>   To send this morning a fat quarter of lamb
>   To a kind gentlewoman in Turnbull Street
>   That longs, and how I'm crost!   II.ii.107–15

A second man with a basket enters, but this one is a friend, the servant of Master Beggarland, who is free with his bribes.

> *First Promoter.* Good Master Oliver? cry thee mercy i'faith!
>   What hast thou there?
> *Man.* A rack of mutton, sir,
>   And half a lamb; you know my mistress' diet.
> *First Promoter.* Go, go, we see thee not; away, keep close!
>   II.ii.119–22

A third character enters—a Country Girl, whose basket conceals her illegitimate child. She begs to be let off, she promises to show "authority" for her mutton, and she leaves the basket with the promoters while she goes to find her master. The promoters, probing the basket, discover first a fat loin of mutton and then the child.

> *Second Promoter.* A child!
> *First Promoter.* A pox of all dissembling cunning whores!
> *Second Promoter.* Here's an unlucky breakfast!
> *First Promoter.* What shall's do?
> *Second Promoter.* The quean made us swear to keep it too.
> *First Promoter.* We might leave it else.
> *Second Promoter.* Villainous strange!

Life, had she none to gull but poor promoters,
That watch hard for a living? II.ii.158–64

The scene of course illustrates Middleton's fondness for tricks,
but it also illustrates his powers of observation and his ability
to make dramatic material out of contemporary rackets.

The scene of the christening is longer and consists, in fact,
of several distinct episodes. First the father dresses, the com-
fit-maker's man appears with a box, the gossips enter the
house and chat, the Puritans expressing the hope that the
child's education may be "pure" and that in time she may
become one of the "faithful." Next the midwife crosses the
stage with the child in her arms, the gossips all following.
At the door little altercations take place. One gossip insists
on entering after her companion, another on entering before,
but the Puritans go in sweetly together.

> *First Puritan.* Come, sweet sister, we go
>   In unity, and show the fruits of peace,
>   Like children of the spirit.
> *Second Puritan.* I love lowliness. [*Exeunt Puritans.*]
> *Fourth Gossip.* True, so say I, though they strive more;
>   There comes as proud behind as goes before.
> *Fifth Gossip.* Every inch, i'faith. [*Exeunt.*]   II.iv.11–16

Finally there is the christening itself. The mother lies in
bed with her child, the gossips grouped about her. The chief
gossip presents the gifts—a silver standing-cup and two
large apostle spoons; the mother thanks him; the comfit-box
circulates. The father, standing at the side of the stage, describes the action that follows:

> Now out comes all the tassell'd handkerchers,
> They're spread abroad between their knees already;
> Now in goes the long fingers that are wash'd
> Some thrice a-day in urine; my wife uses it.
> Now we shall have such pocketing; see how
> They lurch at the lower end! . . .

These women have no consciences at sweetmeats,
Where'er they come; see and they've not cull'd out
All the long plums too, they've left nothing here
But short wriggle-tail comfits, not worth mouthing:
No mar'l I heard a citizen complain once
That his wife's belly only broke his back.   III.ii.51–67

Wine appears and the father is even more outraged.

Now the cups troll about
To wet the gossips' whistles; it pours down, i'faith;
They never think of payment. . . .
Now bless thee, two at once! I'll stay no longer;
It would kill me, and if I paid for it.   III.ii.78–82

The First Puritan repeatedly drinks and hiccoughs. A neighbor's son arrives fresh from Cambridge and the gossips kiss him in turn. The First Puritan, trying to embrace him, staggers and falls to the floor. As she is hoisted up she exclaims:

'Tis but the common affliction of the faithful;
We must embrace our falls.

The father returns, inveigles the gossips out of the house, and comments again:

O, here's a day of toil well pass'd over,
Able to make a citizen hare-mad!
How hot they've made the room with their thick bums!
Dost not feel it, Davy? . . .
Fair needlework stools cost nothing with them, Davy. . . .
Look how they have laid them,
E'en as they lie themselves, with their heels up!
How they have shuffled up the rushes too, Davy,
With their short figging little shittle-cork heels!
These women can let nothing stand as they find it.
                                        .III.ii.180–91

In the exactness of its description the scene is quite masterly; there is nothing comparable to it elsewhere in the drama of the period.

It would be a mistake, however, to overemphasize Middleton's interest in manners, for the core of the play is again an ironic battle of wits—not, as in *A Mad World*, between a young rake on the one hand and a rich old man on the other, but, as in *The Revenger's Tragedy*, between several pairs of characters. Touchwood Junior is pitted against the goldsmith Yellowhammer, whose daughter he wants to marry. He plays three distinct tricks on his antagonist, and the last—the most flagrantly improbable—of the three is completely successful. Tim, the young blockhead from Cambridge, is pitted against the Welshwoman, mistress to Sir Walter Whorehound. Tim is always anxious to show how much he has learned, and he once boasts to his mother that by logic he can prove anything.

> *Maudlin.* What, thou wilt not?
> *Tim.* I'll prove a whore to be an honest woman.
> *Maudlin.* Nay, by my faith, she must prove that herself,
>   Or logic will ne'er do't.
> *Tim.* 'Twill do't, I tell you.
> *Maudlin.* Some in this street would give a thousand pounds
>   That you could prove their wives so.
> *Tim.* Faith, I can,
>   And all their daughters too, though they had three bastards.
>   IV.i.41–47

Like a theme in a symphony, the subject recurs at the end of the play when Tim finds himself married to the Welshwoman.

> *Maudlin.* I think you have married her in logic, Tim.
>   You told me once by logic you would prove
>   A whore an honest woman; prove her so, Tim,
>   And take her for thy labour.
> *Tim.* Troth, I thank you:
>   I grant you, I may prove another man's wife so,
>   But not mine own.   V.iv.95–100

Touchwood Senior, who begets so many children that he is obliged to separate from his wife, is pitted against Sir Oliver Kix, who can beget no children at all. The episode dramatizes a favorite notion of Middleton's—that only the poor, who can ill afford offspring, are prolific. Touchwood sells Sir Oliver a cure for barrenness and at the same time cuckolds him. A child is conceived and Sir Oliver is beside himself with joy.

> Ho, my wife's quicken'd; I'm a man for ever!
> I think I have bestirr'd my stumps, i'faith.   V.iii.1–2

He orders his servants to ring the church bells and to build a bonfire before his door at night.

But the most daring and most ironical of all the wit contests in the play is that between Sir Walter Whorehound and Allwit, his wittol. Sir Walter keeps Allwit's wife, pays all the expenses of the household, educates the sons at Eton, and even takes upon himself the natural jealousy of a husband. Allwit is entirely satisfied:

>   I'm at his table:
> He gets me all my children, and pays the nurse
> Monthly or weekly; puts me to nothing, rent,
> Nor church-duties, not so much as the scavenger:
> The happiest state that ever man was born to!
> I walk out in a morning; come to breakfast,
> Find excellent cheer; a good fire in winter;
> Look in my coal-house about midsummer eve,
> That's full, five or six chaldron new laid up;
> Look in my back-yard, I shall find a steeple
> Made up with Kentish faggots, which o'erlooks
> The water-house and the windmills: I say nothing,
> But smile and pin the door. When she lies in,
> As now she's even upon the point of grunting,
> A lady lies not in like her; there's her embossings,
> Embroiderings, spanglings, and I know not what,

As if she lay with all the gaudy-shops
In Gresham's Burse about her; then her restoratives,
Able to set up a young pothecary,
And richly stock the foreman of a drug-shop;
Her sugar by whole loaves, her wines by rundlets.
I see these things, but, like a happy man,
I pay for none at all; yet fools think's mine;
I have the name, and in his gold I shine.   I.ii.17–40

He has only one worry—that Sir Walter may marry and with-
draw his support—and in the course of the play this almost
happens. He does his best to ward off the catastrophe, when
suddenly an even more devastating catastrophe befalls
him. Sir Walter, seriously wounded in a duel, repents, for-
swears his mistress, disowns his children, and refuses to leave
them anything but curses in his will. He seems to be ready to
lead a better life, Allwit seems about to be exposed and
ruined. But with ironic swiftness the situation changes. It
is reported that Sir Walter's opponent in the duel has died of
his wounds, and Sir Walter seems certain to lose his property
and possibly his life as well. He is obliged to ask Allwit for
sanctuary, but Allwit promptly refuses—he is far too high-
principled to shelter a penniless fugitive.

> *Allwit.* I wonder what he makes here with his consorts?
>   Cannot our house be private to ourselves,
>   But we must have such guests? I pray, depart, sirs,
>   And take your murderer along with you;
>   Good he were apprehended ere he go,
>   Has kill'd some honest gentleman; send for officers.
> *Sir Walter.* I'll soon save you that labour.
> *Allwit.* I must tell you, sir,
>   You have been somewhat bolder in my house
>   Than I could well like of; I suffer'd you
>   Till it stuck here at my heart; I tell you truly
>   I thought y'had been familiar with my wife once.

Mistress Allwit. With me! I'll see him hang'd first; I defy him,
    And all such gentlemen in the like extremity.   V.i.136–48

And so Sir Walter is carried off to meet his fate—actually imprisonment for debt—while the Allwits remain behind to lay plans for a comfortable future.

Allwit. . . . What shall we do now, wife?
Mistress Allwit. As we were wont to do.
Allwit. We're richly furnish'd, wife,
    With household stuff.
Mistress Allwit. Let's let out lodgings then,
    And take a house in the Strand.
Allwit. In troth, a match, wench!
    We're simply stock'd with cloth-of-tissue cushions
    To furnish out bay-windows; push, what not
    That's quaint and costly, from the top to the bottom;
    Life, for furniture we may lodge a countess.   V.i.156–63

From the standpoint of morality the triumph of Allwit is perhaps a little more disturbing than the triumph of Sir Bounteous Progress in *A Mad World, My Masters* and the triumph of Witgood in *A Trick to Catch the Old One*, and yet it is entirely consistent with Middleton's point of view. In his ironic comedies he is always concerned with contests between pairs of scoundrels, both pretty hopelessly depraved, both moved by a desire either for money or "mutton"; and in the end he always represents one scoundrel as successful at the expense of the other. There are no courtroom scenes in these plays, as there are in *Phoenix* and *Michaelmas Term*, no dispassionate judges who come forward at the last minute to administer poetic justice. There is retribution, no doubt, but since it overtakes only one of each pair of scoundrels, it is perhaps less impressive and less terrifying than it should be. The fact is that Middleton is a realist as well as a moralist. He is willing and even eager to show that cleverness overreaches itself and that unscrupulous men are usually themselves betrayed, but he is not willing to distribute rewards and punishments in a completely unrealistic way. And since realism involves letting some of his scoundrels off, he accepts the situation and laughs. There are few scenes in *A Chaste Maid* more uproariously amusing than the one in which the Allwits count their gains.

A good deal has recently been made of the harshness of Middleton's attitude toward human nature in the play, as though he had suddenly realized for the first time that he was dealing with a repulsive world,[2] but to me at least this harshness is never very clearly reflected in the text. It is no doubt true that the characters are an ugly lot, but the same can be said of the characters in the other city comedies. It is also true that there is a good deal of vulgarity shown in the play—in the christening scenes, for example, where the gossips get drunk and belch, and cause such acute distress to the sensitive Allwit. Yet there is no reason to suppose that Middleton shares this distress, or that he represents it for any purpose other than to create laughter. He seems to me, in short, as light-hearted in *A Chaste Maid* as he is in *A Mad World*, and quite as ready to tolerate human depravity. He again faces society and again finds it amusing—finds it amusing for almost the last time in his career, before the mood of *The Revenger's Tragedy* grows on him and he becomes absorbed in sombre studies of sin and weakness.

II

Middleton's next comedy, *No Wit, No Help Like a Woman's*, is not only inferior to *A Chaste Maid*, it is entirely different. It is a potboiler, an exercise in the fashionable manner of

---

[2] U. M. Ellis-Fermor, *The Jacobean Drama* (London, 1936), pp. 135–38, and L. C. Knights, *Drama & Society in the Age of Jonson* (London, 1937), p. 269, note.

Beaumont and Fletcher, an attempt to exploit the conventions of Jacobean romance. The scene is indeed London, but there is scarcely a suggestion of London manners; the characters and the incidents come from literature and not from life. Yet if one accepts the play for what it is, if one regards it as an unpretentious collection of farcical and melodramatic scenes, one can scarcely deny that it achieves a measure of success.

One story, patently of Latin derivation, concerns the attempts of a young man to pass off his wife as his long-lost sister. The attempts are at first amusing, especially in the scenes in which the principal part is played by Savourwit, the intriguing servant of Latin comedy. Later there is pathos of a sort, for it appears that the wife is indeed the sister, and in the last acts the young man is overwhelmed by a sense of guilt and a horror of incest. But naturally the relationships straighten themselves out in the final scene. The other story is equally conventional and equally dramatic. An impoverished wife tries to recover her money from Lady Goldenfleece, a rich widow who has appropriated it. She dresses as a man, marries her enemy, and succeeds on the wedding night —after she has haled the widow and the poor scholar of the play out of a bedroom. The comic character is here Weatherwise, a foolish eccentric who lives by the almanac, and the most amusing scene is the one in which Weatherwise entertains Lady Goldenfleece at a banquet. The dishes resemble the twelve signs of the zodiac, and the cup in which the wine is served looks like the sun—at least it is described in the dialogue as a "sun-cup." The wit, which is appropriately astronomical, is as conceited and ingenious as anything in Lyly. The play as a whole never suggests that Middleton's proper medium was romantic comedy, but it certainly shows that he could if he tried write smart plays more or less of the Beaumont and Fletcher kind.

The Widow is an even smarter performance and one that is occasionally reminiscent of the earlier Middleton. There is a jealous husband who helps his wife make an assignation with her lover and later helps the lover to keep it. The whole situation is of course ironical, and in one scene at least the irony is heavily underscored. Francisco, the lover, has just been arrested, and Brandino, the husband, is urged to bail him out.

> *Martino.* Have you forgot so soon what he did lately? . . .
>   Shall it be said, I serve an ingrateful master?
> *Brandino.* Never, Martino; I will bail him now,
>   And 'twere at my wife's suit.
> *Francisco.* [*Aside.*] 'Tis like to be so.   II.ii.157–63

When Francisco is free the husband continues:

> Fare thee well once again, my dear Francisco;
>   I prithee, use my house.
> *Francisco.* It is my purpose, sir.   II.ii.174–75

And so Francisco rides off to keep his appointment. There are also amusing examples of irony in the scenes of the thieves and in the scenes of the unfortunate Martia, who blunders through the play in breeches. In fact, Middleton almost succeeds in making a really distinguished comedy out of conventional romantic material—almost but not quite, I think. *The Widow* is much frothier and less substantial than the city comedies, with which it invites comparison. In the quarto edition of the play the names of Fletcher and Jonson appear, along with Middleton's, on the title-page. Fletcher might well have sketched the plot and Jonson has been suspected of helping with the scene in which Latrocinio disguises himself as an "empiric," but the dialogue seems to be entirely, or almost entirely, Middleton's.

Wit at Several Weapons, which should perhaps be considered a play of doubtful authorship, is less romantic than *The Widow* and even closer to Middleton's early work. The main plot concerns Sir Perfidious Oldcraft, a great admirer of wit. In his youth he lived by wit—by pimping and swindling orphans—and now he expects his son to do likewise. The son, whose name is Wittypate, does so. He brings off three successful tricks, but all are at the expense of his father. The irony is a little like that in *A Mad World, My Masters*, where wit is made to recoil upon itself. The best scene is the one in which Wittypate stands by while his companions extort money from Sir Perfidious on the pretense that his nephew has just robbed them. Wittypate has the effrontery to offer his help, but the old knight brushes him aside.

Old Knight. . . . Go, go, live by your wits, go.
Wittypate. I practise all I can.   IV, p. 111

Later the nephew—who actually thinks himself guilty—gets an ironical lecture from Wittypate, the very man who, in the disguise of a thief, persuaded him to take part in the mock robbery.

Wittypate. Oh fie Cozen,
    These are ill courses, you a Scholar too?
Credulous. I was drawn into't most unfortunately,
    By filthy deboist company.
Wittypate. I, I, I.
    'Tis even the spoil of all our youth in *England*.
    What were they Gentlemen?
Credulous. Faith so like some on 'em,
    They were ev'n the worse agen.
Wittypate. Hum.
Credulous. Great Tobacco [swivers],
    They would go near to rob with a pipe in their mouths.
Wittypate. What, no?
Credulous. Faith leave it Cozen, because my Rascals use it.
                                        IV, pp. 111–12

This is very much like Middleton's best comic work, but there are other scenes in which he is not nearly so good and still others which are not his at all. For in *Wit at Several*

Weapons he certainly worked with a collaborator, who may not have been either Beaumont or Fletcher, even though the play originally appeared in the Beaumont and Fletcher folio.

The last of Middleton's comedies, *Anything for a Quiet Life,* is also very probably a product of collaboration. The main plot, which seems to be Webster's, is rather serious and very silly; the underplot, which is Middleton's, is entirely frivolous. There is something about a barber named Sweetball, who uses a preposterous professional lingo—as amusing in its way as the lingo of Jonson's alchemists—and who tries to operate for the pox on a quite virtuous and healthy young man. The *doubles-entendres* in the scene are uproariously funny and outrageously indecent. There is also something about a young sharper who escapes arrest by speaking French and striking up an acquaintanceship with a Frenchwoman who conveniently appears. It is all very lively farce, but one hesitates to give it the very highest praise because it is mere farce, not obviously related either to life or Middleton's view of life.

A survey of Middleton's later comedy should perhaps include remarks about the comic scenes in the plays that are predominantly serious, but there are not really very many of them that deserve consideration. The witch scenes in the play called *The Witch* and the Dondolo scenes in *More Dissemblers Besides Women* are obviously perfunctory. The doctor scenes in *A Fair Quarrel* are almost exactly the same as the comedy of Sweetball in *Anything for a Quiet Life.* The scenes of the Ward in *Women Beware Women* are effective in their context but scarcely interesting apart from it. The scenes of Simon in *Hengist, King of Kent* are indeed an exception. They are very brilliant in themselves, though, oddly enough, inappropriate in their context and somewhat in the manner of Middleton's most persistent collaborator, William Rowley. I shall have a word or two to say about them later.

The picture of Middleton that emerges from a study of the later comedy is a decidedly curious one, that of a dramatic hack who turns his hand to whatever sort of work seems at the moment most likely to please. If a play in the manner of Beaumont and Fletcher is wanted, Middleton writes it and the result is *No Wit, No Help Like a Woman's*. If a comic part in the manner of Rowley is in demand at the theatre, Middleton turns it out and the result is the character of Simon, Mayor of Quinborough. He is even capable of producing scenes more or less in his own early manner, though —after *A Chaste Maid in Cheapside* at least—no whole play in which his comic brilliance is sustained. This is the picture, but fortunately not the complete picture. To get the rest of it we must turn to the tragedies and tragicomedies, where Middleton's interest is really engaged and where he tries to create a new sort of serious drama, different from but by no means inferior to the drama of the city comedies.

CHAPTER VI

Tragicomedies

WITH the exception of *A Game at Chess*, Middleton's tragicomedies seem to have been written in the second decade of the seventeenth century, perhaps between 1613 and 1618. All are "romantic" plays and all are to some extent artificial; all have improbable plots, inappropriate comic scenes, and preposterous happy endings. Yet all contain, despite their obvious artificiality, suggestions of a much more impressive sort of drama, not quite tragedy perhaps but something very much like it. All emphasize human weakness, all dwell on the tragic irony that defeats human desires, all portray a dark world—less violent perhaps but scarcely less terrifying than the world of *The Revenger's Tragedy* and *Women Beware Women*. To interpret these plays is almost inevitably to distort them—to single out the more serious elements and to slight the rest. Yet I cannot help feeling that this is the right critical procedure. The task of the student, as I see it, is to fix attention on what in each play is characteristically Middleton's and to state as far as possible his individual point of view, even though in the play as a whole this point of view may not always be perfectly expressed.

I

The Witch is the least interesting play in the group, and the closest to the Beaumont and Fletcher formula. It is really a companion piece to *No Wit*, a decidedly unscrupulous work in which the author relies almost entirely on the stock situations of the romantic stage. One of the chief characters is a Duchess who objects—as well she might—to the Duke's habit of using her father's skull as a drinking cup and so decides to murder him. She arranges an assignation with a young man who has never aspired to her favors and who, in fact, has been making advances to her woman. She blindfolds him and keeps him in complete ignorance of what is in store for him, so that when he appears on the stage—still blindfolded—he chatters complacently about what he takes to be the hypocrisy of his mistress:

> This you that was a maid? how are you born
> To deceive men! I'd thought to have married you:
> I had been finely handled, had I not?
> I'll say that man is wise ever hereafter
> That tries his wife beforehand. 'Tis no marvel
> You should profess such bashfulness, to blind one,
> As if you durst not look a man i' th' face,
> Your modesty would blush so. Why do you not run
> And tell the duchess now? go; you should tell all:
> Let her know this too.   III.i.1–10

At this point the Duchess removes the bandage from his eyes and, with Websterian suddenness, confronts him with the alternative of killing the Duke or dying himself. The stagecraft is masterly but it leads nowhere. The Duke is not killed, and it even appears in the end that the Duchess has not really compromised herself.

Another character is Sebastian, who returns after three years' absence just in time to get a charm from the witches and thus prevent the consummation of his mistress's marriage. The story is involved, melodramatic, and quite unconvincing. The witches, who appear in three scenes, are an obvious attempt on Middleton's part to exploit the popular interest in the supernatural. They do a good many of the things that witches are said to do in Reginald Scot—brew up dead children, melt wax images, fly through the air, and dance around caldrons. It is characteristic of Middleton that they are very much interested in sex:

> *Firestone.* . . . Mother, I pray, give me leave to ramble
> abroad tonight with the Nightmare, for I have a great mind
> to overlay a fat parson's daughter.
> *Hecate.* And who shall lie with me, then?
> *Firestone.* The great cat
> For one night, mother; 'tis but a night:
> Make shift with him for once.
> *Hecate.* You're a kind son!
> But 'tis the nature of you all, I see that;
> You had rather hunt after strange women still
> Than lie with your own mothers. I.ii.90–98

But despite their eccentric relationships, they are never much more than dramatic illustrations of the books on demonology.

In only one thread of his complicated plot does Middleton really succeed in expressing himself, that involving the characters of Francisca and Aberzanes. Francisca, the more notable of the two, is a girl who at the age of sixteen has a lover and is about to have a child. Like many of Middleton's characters, she introduces herself in soliloquy.

These bastards come upon poor venturing gentlewomen ten to one faster than your legitimate children: if I had been married, I'll be hanged if I had been with child so soon now. When they are our husbands, they'll be whipt ere they take such pains as a friend will do; to come by water to the back-door at midnight, there stay perhaps an hour in all weathers, with a pair of reeking watermen laden with bottles of wine, chewets, and currant-custards. I may curse those egg-pies, they are meat that help forward too fast. II.i.43–52

Later in the same scene her sister-in-law urges her to marry.

> *Isabella.* These good offices,
> If you had a husband, you might exercise,

To th' good o' th' commonwealth, and so much profit:
Beside, it is a comfort to a woman
T' have children, sister; a great blessing certainly.
Francisca. They will come fast enough.
Isabella. Not so fast neither
  As they're still welcome to an honest woman.
Francisca. [*Aside.*] How near she comes to me! I protest she
                          grates
  My very skin.
Isabella. Were I conceiv'd with child,
  Beshrew my heart, I should be so proud on't!
Francisca. That's natural; pride is a kind of swelling:—
  [*Aside.*] But yet I've small cause to be proud of mine.

II.i.89–100

Treated a little more genially, Francisca might well have been a character in one of the early comedies. She might have brought off a successful trick and might thus have disposed of her child—she might, in fact, have gulled a pair of promoters as did the Country Girl in *A Chaste Maid in Cheapside*. But Francisca is not treated genially at all—she is an appalling example of juvenile depravity—and accordingly she is exposed and lectured. Her lover, Aberzanes, is a dastardly and tightfisted fop. When the child is born, he has it left surreptitiously on his tailor's porch. "I love to get 'em," he says, "but not to keep 'em."

                    It's well for the boy too;
He'll get an excellent trade by't; and on Sundays
Go like a gentleman that has pawn'd his rapier:
He need not care what countryman his father was,
Nor what his mother was when he was gotten:
The boy will do well certain: give him grace
To have a quick hand and convey things cleanly!

II.iii.16–22

Before the play ends Aberzanes is properly forced, at the point of a sword, to marry his whore.

Both Francisca and Aberzanes reflect the bitter realism of Middleton's later drama, and the same can perhaps be said of the four principal characters in *More Dissemblers Besides Women*—the Duchess, the Cardinal, Lactantio, and Aurelia. For all are hypocrites, and all are involved at one time or another in brazen deceptions. Furthermore, all are to some extent the victims of their own cleverness. They try to deceive others but they actually deceive themselves; they suffer the same kind of ironic retribution as that which overtakes such earlier characters as Follywit and Hoard.

The Duchess, the only one of the four to receive sympathetic treatment, is a widow who has taken a vow of chastity and for seven years has faithfully kept it. But when, to make her triumph even greater, the Cardinal insists that she appear in public, she at once falls hopelessly in love with her general, Andrugio, almost the first man whom she sees. The scene shifts to her dressing-room, where she is giving instructions to Celia, her maid.

> *Duchess.* Seek out the lightest colours can be got,
> The youthfull'st dressings; tawny is too sad,
> I am not thirty yet; I've wrong'd my time
> To go so long in black, like a petitioner:
> See that the powder that I use about me
> Be rich in cassia.
> *Celia.* Here's a sudden change! [*Aside.*]   II.i.1–6

A change indeed, almost as great as the change in the Country Wench of *Michaelmas Term*, who also appears in a dressing-room flaunting her finery, but the motive is here really love, not lust or greed. The Duchess struggles with her weakness, and when the Cardinal comes in to congratulate her, she asks him to repeat with her the last words of her dying husband. But when she reaches the beginning of the vow, she stops.

> *Cardinal.* Why, madam!
> *Duchess.* I can go no further.

Cardinal. What,
   Have you forgot your vow?
Duchess. I have, too certainly.
Cardinal. Your vow? that cannot be; it follows now
   Just where I left.
Duchess. My frailty gets before it;
   Nothing prevails but ill.
Cardinal. What ail you, madam?
Duchess. Sir, I'm in love.
Cardinal. O, all you powers of chastity,
   Look to this woman! let her not faint now,
   For honour of yourselves! If she be lost,
   I know not where to seek my hope in woman.
   Madam, O madam!
Duchess. My desires are sicken'd
   Beyond recovery of good counsel, sir.   II.i.88–98

She goes on to complete her confession, but she names, not
Andrugio, but Lactantio, the Cardinal's nephew. It later
appears that she intends to use Lactantio. She persuades him
to write a love-letter addressed to herself and to sign it with
Andrugio's name. She then arrests Andrugio, confronts him
with the letter, and accuses him of conspiring to break her
vow. He of course denies that the letter is his.

Duchess. Fie, fie, deny your hand?
   I will not deny mine; here, take it freely, sir,
   And with it, my true constant heart for ever:
   I never disgrac'd man that sought my favour.
Andrugio. What mean you, madam?
Duchess. To requite you, sir;
   By courtesy I hold my reputation,
   And you shall taste it. Sir, in as plain truth
   As the old time walk'd in, when love was simple
   And knew no art nor guile, I affect you;
   My heart has made her choice: I love you, sir,
   Above my vow: the frown that met you first
   Wore not the livery of anger, sir,

But of deep policy; I made your enemy
The instrument for all; there you may praise me,
And 'twill not be ill given.   IV.ii.180–94

The scene is remarkably similar to the scene in which the
Duchess of Malfi confesses her love to Antonio. Similar but
at the same time quite different; for Webster's Duchess is
married at once, while Middleton's can only discover a bitter
truth—that Andrugio is himself in love with a younger
woman. The discovery is tragic—or should be—and Middleton just fails, I think, to realize its full implications. He has
his character take it quite calmly, even perhaps a little prig-
gishly:

> *Duchess.* I confess
> I have no wrong at all; she's younger, fairer;
> He has not now dishonour'd me in choice;
> I much commend his noble care and judgment;
> 'Twas a just cross led in by a temptation,
> For offering but to part from my dear vow,
> And I'll embrace it cheerfully.   V.ii.127–33

Middleton does not so fail with Lady Ager, the central
character in *A Fair Quarrel,* who is fully aware of her own
tragedy, never more so than in her final words.

It is perhaps an overstatement to call the Duchess a hypocrite. She is a beautiful and warmly human character, whose
only fault is that she misjudges the strength of her own quite
natural and entirely human passions. But about the hypocrisy
of the Cardinal there can no possible doubt. He prates about
chastity, he writes volumes in praise of the Duchess, he itches
to show her off in public. But when she tells him that she is
in love with his nephew, he at once sacrifices his principles.
He proves, by elaborate casuistry, that chastity is not a virtue
after all: the Duchess is almost obliged to marry Lactantio.

> Can chastity be any whit impair'd
> By that which makes it perfect? answer, madam;

> Do you profess constancy, and yet live alone?
> How can that hold? you're constant then to none;
> That's a dead virtue.   IV.ii.24–28

Middleton's comment is placed in the mouth of the Duchess:

> O, there's no art like a religious cunning,
> It carries away all things smooth before it!   IV.ii.51–52

The nephew, Lactantio, is another Aberzanes—a "perfum'd parcel of curl'd powder'd hair." Before his uncle he passes as a model of chastity, but he is actually an impudent and cynical whoremaster. He abandons one mistress for Aurelia, and Aurelia for the Duchess, only to overreach himself. In the end he is caught in the net of his own deceptions. Aurelia, the fourth hypocrite, is almost as young and quite as much of a minx as Francisca in *The Witch*. A few lines are perhaps sufficient to illustrate her character:

> I have undone myself
> Two ways at once; lost a great deal of time,
> And now I'm like to lose more. O my fortune!
> I was nineteen yesterday, and partly vow'd
> To have a child by twenty, if not twain:
> To see how maids are cross'd!   V.ii.153–58

Another important character is the Page, Lactantio's disguised mistress, who is sometimes reminiscent of Beaumont's Bellario. It is perhaps a measure of the difference between Beaumont's genius and Middleton's that, whereas Bellario reveals her identity when she is about to be tortured, the Page reveals hers when she gives birth to a bastard in the middle of a dancing lesson.

More Dissemblers Besides Women is certainly not a great play, but it has what all the "romantic" plays so far considered really lack—a point of view. It creates a world of weak or despicable characters who, in their blindness, undo themselves for ends that they can never attain. The Duchess violates her vow for a man who is already in love; Lactantio abandons his mistress for a woman who never even considers him as a husband; the Cardinal gives up the most deeply cherished principle of his religion for a marriage that can never take place. The irony is the same as that found in *A Trick to Catch the Old One* and *A Chaste Maid in Cheapside*, but the mood of the author is entirely different, for in this case he takes a much more serious view of human frailty.

II

The Old Law and *A Fair Quarrel*, two plays that contain serious stories somewhat like the story of the Duchess in *More Dissemblers Besides Women*, were written by Middleton in collaboration, the first with Rowley and possibly Massinger, the second with Rowley alone.

William Rowley was an actor-playwright who specialized in melodrama and farce. The melodrama is nothing if not Jacobean. It is always absurdly violent and usually involves a physical clash between simple but strongly marked personalities. When they are thoroughly aroused, his characters are quite likely to spit at one another. The farce, which usually concerns punning clowns, has all the faults and a few of the merits of the Launce scenes in Shakespeare. But whatever his literary limitations, Rowley knew the stage, and it was apparently for this reason that he was often invited to collaborate with the more distinguished dramatists of his time. When he worked with Middleton, he usually wrote the farcical or melodramatic subplots. But he also had a hand in the main plots, at the beginning at least, and according to one theory, he revised all of the dialogue. It may be significant that the later Middleton is nowhere so direct and concise as in two of the plays in which Rowley was concerned—*A Fair Quarrel* and *The Changeling*.[1]

[1] Some scholars—Arthur Symons, for example—believe that Rowley made important contributions to these plays and that such characters as Captain Ager and De Flores are the product of close collaboration. Of

The central situation in *The Old Law* is wildly fantastic. The Duke of Epire has decided, for the good of the commonwealth, to put to death all women who have reached the age of sixty and all men who have reached the age of eighty. The decision is acceptable to the relatives of many of the condemned, but quite unacceptable to others. Some of the scenes are serious, some comic, and some entirely farcical. It is perhaps impossible to determine exactly where one author leaves off and another begins, but Rowley seems principally responsible for the first act and the farce, Middleton for the central scenes, the core of the play.

The Middleton scenes—in so far as they can be considered apart from their context—are essentially concerned with tragic weakness. They tell the ironic story of the unfortunate Hippolita, who betrays herself and her family, but who is nevertheless always moved by the very highest motives. For throughout the play she is represented as the perfect wife, the joy of her husband, and the delight of her father-in-law Leonides. In fact, when Leonides is sentenced to death under the Duke's law, he scarcely remembers his own misfortune; he is lost in admiration of Hippolita's virtues.

> *Leonides.* Death! what's that, Cleanthes? I thought not on't,
> I was in contemplation of this woman:
> 'Tis all thy comfort, son; thou hast in her
> A treasure unvaluable, keep her safe.
> When I die, sure 'twill be a gentle death,
> For I will die with wonder of her virtues;
> Nothing else shall dissolve me.
> *Cleanthes.* 'Twere much better, sir,

Women Beware Women Symons says: ". . . the heights of *The Changeling*, the nobility of even what was evil in the passions of that play, are no longer attained. Middleton, left to himself, has returned, with new experience and new capacity, to his own level" (*Cambridge History of English Literature*, Cambridge, 1932, VI, 79). But it is not clear to me that the characters in *The Changeling* are much nobler than those in Middleton's unassisted plays.

    Could you prevent their malice.
Leonides. I'll prevent 'em,
    And die the way I told thee, in the wonder
    Of this good woman.   I.i.356–65

In this course of the scene she fully justifies this high opinion.
She insists that Leonides take steps to escape execution, and
she and her husband, Cleanthes, finally arrange to con-
ceal him in a remote lodge and to report in public that he is
dead. The scheme seems foolproof since only Hippolita and
Cleanthes share the secret. Hippolita is indeed a woman;
but, she says,

    You must not mistrust my faith, though my sex plead
    Weak[ness] and frailty for me.   I.i.461–62

Leonides is concealed, his funeral is celebrated, and Hippolita later goes to visit a relative, Eugenia—her exact opposite in every respect, one of the minxes of Middleton's later
drama. Eugenia is married to an old man, but it is already
clear that she has no intention whatever of saving him from
execution under the law.

    The mere conceit turns a young woman's stomach.
    His slippers must be warm'd, in August too,
    And his gown girt to him in the very dog-days,
    When every mastiff lolls out's tongue for heat.
    Would not this vex a beauty of nineteen now?
    Alas! I should be tumbling in cold baths now,
    Under each armpit a fine bean-flower bag,
    To screw out whiteness when I list—
    And some seven of the properest men i'the dukedom
    Making a banquet ready i'the next room for me.

                                  II.ii.6–15

But Eugenia is an accomplished hypocrite, and in Hippolita's
presence she manages to shed tears over her husband's ap-
proaching fate.

Eugenia. Yours was a father-in-law, but mine a husband:
 O, for a woman that could love, and live
 With an old man, mine is a jewel, cousin;
 So quietly he lies by one, so still!
Hippolita. [*Aside.*] Alas! I have a secret lodg'd within me,
 Which now will out in pity:—I can't hold.
Eugenia. One that will not disturb me in my sleep
 For a whole month together, 'less it be
 With those diseases age is subject to,
 As aches, coughs, and pains, and these, heaven knows,
 Against his will too:—he's the quietest man,
 Especially in bed.   II.ii.154–65

Hippolita is overcome by pity: she can hold out no longer, she must share her secret. "I'm like one," she says,

 Loves not to banquet with a joy alone,
 My friends must partake too.   II.ii.171–73

And so she tells the whole story of Leonides' concealment. Subsequently Eugenia's husband himself tries to circumvent the law. He dances, fences, drinks—anything to appear younger than he is—and at the height of his folly Cleanthes surprises him. Cleanthes is extremely bitter. Such conduct, he says, is like forcing ground

 That has been so long hallow'd like a temple,
 To bring forth fruits of earth now. III.ii.225–26

But Cleanthes is even more bitter toward Eugenia. "Strumpet!" he shouts.

Eugenia. Do you call, sir?
Cleanthes. Whore!
Eugenia. How do you, sir?
Cleanthes. Be I ne'er so well,
 I must be sick of thee; thou'rt a disease
 That stick'st to th'heart,—as all such women are.
         III.ii.265–68

Eugenia now has a motive for revenge, and the weapon is
already in her hands.

The last of the Middleton scenes brings the story to its
inevitable conclusion. Cleanthes stands before the lodge which
conceals his father, afraid yet eager to reassure himself:

> he that hides treasure,
> Imagines every one thinks of that place,
> When 'tis a thing least minded; nay, let him change
> The place continually; where'er it keeps,
> There will the fear keep still: yonder's the store-house
> Of all my comfort now.   IV.ii.17–22

Hippolita enters and he salutes her as the "precious chief of
women." Leonides follows and echoes the praise:

> How sweetly sounds the voice of a good woman!
> It is so seldom heard, that, when it speaks,
> It ravishes all senses.   IV.ii.32–34

The words are almost the same as those which Leonides used
in the first act, but the irony is only now apparent. Hunting
horns sound, Leonides retires, the Duke and his courtiers
appear. Hippolita and Cleanthes stick to their story, but
their secret has already been revealed. Leonides is led away
to execution and they are not even sure that they will see
him before his death to receive his final blessing. In his
agony Cleanthes turns on Hippolita.

> *Cleanthes.* Thou shouldst be good,
>   Or thou'rt a dangerous substance to be lodg'd
>   So near the heart of man.
> *Hippolita.* What means this, dear sir?
> *Cleanthes.* To thy trust only was this blessed secret
>   Kindly committed; 'tis destroy'd, thou seest;
>   What follows to be thought on't?   IV.ii.210–15

Just at this moment Eugenia enters to reveal her triumph.
"I betray['d] him," she says,

And now we're even, you'd best keep you so.
Cleanthes. Is there not poison yet enough to kill me?
Hippolita. O sir, forgive me! it was I betray'd him.
Cleanthes. How!
Hippolita. I.
Cleanthes. The fellow of my heart! 'twill speed me, then.
Hippolita. Her tears that never wept, and mine own pity
   E'en cozen'd me together, and stole from me
  This secret, which fierce death should not have purchas'd.
IV.ii.235–44

Hippolita is right. Her weakness was caused by pity; she has undone herself and her husband by the very virtues that made her so perfect a wife.

The fifth act brings about the conventional happy ending, but though Middleton was quite capable of planning it—as he shows in *A Fair Quarrel*—he does not seem in this case to have written it himself. *The Old Law* is certainly not one of his most successful plays. Hippolita is lost in a crowded canvas, and she is not, in any case, much of a character. But her tragedy is, in conception at least, a real tragedy, one that anticipates in many respects the deeper and more moving tragedy of Lady Ager.

In *A Fair Quarrel* it is, or seems to be, fairly easy to separate the work of the collaborators. The comic scenes, the underplot, and the first scene of the main plot are almost certainly Rowley's; the main plot after the first scene is almost certainly Middleton's. The chief character in the main plot is again a woman—in this case, a soldier's mother—who is weak, but never unscrupulous, and whose only concern is to save her son from foolishly risking his life. Yet she fails even when she lies, even indeed when she tells the truth. Her anguish is another example of the tragic misfortune that overtakes entirely virtuous people, of the tragic irony that is rooted, not only in depravity, but in virtue itself.

The son, Captain Ager, suddenly becomes involved in a quarrel with the Colonel of the play, who has always been one of his closest friends. He tries to avoid the quarrel when he sees it developing, and he behaves throughout with admirable restraint, but in the end he is called the son of a whore. He prepares to fight as his code demands: his mother's honor as well as his own is at stake. But—unlike many similar characters in later Jacobean drama—he is concerned about his soul as well as about his honor, and he is determined, before he fights, to make quite sure that his cause is just.[2] "The son of a whore?" he says,

> There is not such another murdering-piece
> In all the stock of calumny; it kills
> At one report two reputations,
> A mother's and a son's.   II.i.1–5

But, he continues,

> I am too full of conscience,
> Knowledge and patience, to give justice to't;
> So careful of my eternity, which consists
> Of upright actions, that unless I knew
> It were a truth I stood for, any coward
> Might make my breast his foot-pace: and who lives
> That can assure the truth of his conception,
> More than a mother's carriage makes it hopeful?
> And is't not miserable valour then,
> That men should hazard all upon things doubtful?
>   II.i.9–18

Still there is only one person who can resolve the doubt, his mother, and he accordingly tells her the story of the quarrel without suggesting that he himself is obliged to

[2] Cf. *The Peacemaker* in Bullen, VIII, 339, where Middleton says: ". . . true fortitude distinguisheth of the grounds of quarrels, whether they be just. . . ." But in *The Peacemaker* he argues against all duelling.

avenge the insult. But when he reaches the words "son of a whore," she strikes him; her deepest feelings are outraged. "This is no question to be slighted off," she says,

> And at your pleasure clos'd up fair again,
> As though you'd never touch'd it: no, honour doubted
> Is honour deeply wounded; and it rages
> More than a common smart, being of thy making;
> For thee to fear my truth, it kills my comfort:
> Where should fame seek for her reward, when he
> That is her own by the great tie of blood,
> Is farthest off in bounty? O poor goodness!
> That only pay'st thyself with thy own works,
> For nothing else looks towards thee.   II.i.97–107

Overjoyed—for there can be no possible doubt of her sincerity—Captain Ager reveals his own share in the quarrel and prepares to leave for the field of honor. But suddenly his mother stops him. She is at last fully aware of the tragic choice that confronts her, she at last realizes that she must sacrifice her own honor if she is to prevent her son from risking his life. She makes the choice, she pretends to confess that he is really a bastard, and she leaves him utterly dejected and quite incapable—or so she thinks—of going through with the duel.

But even her pretended confession is not enough to keep a soldier from what he takes to be his duty. The Captain goes to the field, temporizes, and carefully waits until the Colonel calls him a coward; then and only then he springs into action, for then he knows that he has a just cause. He draws his sword, exchanges a few passes with his adversary, and leaves him, desperately wounded, on the field. His mother, in the meantime, sends one servant after another to find him. She hears that he has gone with his seconds and she is afraid that he has already been killed. "Wretched affection!" she exclaims,

> Have I belied my faith, injur'd my goodness,
> Slander'd my honour for his preservation,
> Having but only him, and yet no happier? . . .
> Run, seek away! if there be any hope,
> Let me not lose him yet. When I think on him,
> His dearness and his worth, it earns me more:
> They that know riches tremble to be poor.   III.iii.19–40

At last he returns and she runs to him, calling for a surgeon. She can scarcely believe that he has not been wounded, and he in his turn—when she retracts her falsehood—can scarcely believe that she is now speaking the truth. Both are finally convinced, both are entirely happy. But a moment later the conflict between them breaks out again. The Captain decides that he must fight a second time—

>   O my glory,
> Why, this, this is the quarrel that I look'd for!
> The other but a shift to hold time play—

and he utters a fervent prayer that his enemy's life may be spared. His mother turns from him reproachfully, her anxiety as great as ever. "What an unhappiness have I in goodness!" she exclaims.

> 'Tis ever my desire to intend well,
> But have no fortunate way in't. For all this
> Deserve I yet no better of you
> But to be griev'd again? Are you not well
> With honest gain of fame, with safety purchas'd?
> Will you needs tempt a ruin that avoids you?   IV.iii.83–89

This is not quite her last appearance in the play, but she never speaks again.

A good deal has been made in recent criticism of the conscientious scruples of the Captain, and it has even been said that *A Fair Quarrel* is a kind of Jacobean problem play on the subject of the dueling code. But surely this is wrong.

It is like calling *Ghosts* a problem play on the subject of syphilis or *The Cherry Orchard* a problem play on the subject of mortgages. *A Fair Quarrel* is really a tragedy; not perhaps a Jacobean tragedy, for no one dies and there is not much violence, but a bourgeois tragedy of a type not uncommon in more modern times. The central character is a woman—a quite ordinary woman, in fact, like Ibsen's Mrs. Alving—who tries to keep her son from harm. But she fails and she realizes that she will always fail; she knows that she can never be sure, from hour to hour, that he will not risk his life in some silly quarrel. The son is less important and distinctly less credible. His behavior is priggish early in the play—as indeed it must be if he is to go to his mother with the story of the quarrel—but he is never allowed to become an unsympathetic character.

Ibsen might have conceived the tragedy of Lady Ager, and Ibsen in fact might have written much of the dialogue. For though the speeches are occasionally long and highly metaphorical, they are more often short, prosaic, and terse. An extreme example is the passage in which Lady Ager first realizes that she must lie if she is to prevent her son from fighting the Colonel.

Lady Ager. Stay, I say!

Captain Ager. In anything command me but in this, madam.

Lady Ager. [*Aside.*] 'Las, I shall lose him!—You will hear me first?

Captain Ager. At my return I will.

Lady Ager. You'll never hear me more, then.

Captain Ager. How?

Lady Ager. Come back, I say!

You may well think there's cause I call so often.

Captain Ager. Ha, cause! what cause?

Lady Ager. So much, you must not go.

Captain Ager. How?

Lady Ager. You must not go.

Captain Ager. Must not! why?
Lady Ager. I know a reason for't,
    Which I could wish you'd yield to, and not know;
    If not, it must come forth: faith, do not know,
    And yet obey my will.   II.i.148–61

Dialogue of this sort would scarcely be out of place in *Rosmersholm* or *The Wild Duck*.

A Fair Quarrel is not as a whole much better than the other romantic plays; Rowley is too prominent in it and even Middleton is not always at his best. The happy ending—the repentance of the Colonel and the marriage between his sister and the Captain—completely destroys the mood that the author has carefully built up. But if one confines one's attention to the story of the Agers, and in particular to the two great scenes between mother and son, one can scarcely deny that the play is one of the triumphs of the Jacobean theatre, written by a man who is himself not quite a Jacobean, who is almost as close to Ibsen as to Webster and Shakespeare.

CHAPTER VII

Later Tragedies

IN the best scenes of his tragicomedies Middleton shows an interest in psychology that is difficult to parallel in his early work or in the work of his contemporaries. He explores the minds of his characters, he creates an inner drama that is quite as important as the drama actually seen on the stage. "Compared with the characters of earlier plays," Miss Bradbrook says, "Middleton's are fuller, more natural and human." [1] But in his poorer scenes—and there are examples even in *A Fair Quarrel*—he completely ignores character and resorts to a drama of pure intrigue. It is for this reason, of course, that the tragicomedies can seldom be praised without qualification. They are very brilliant in certain scenes and entirely perfunctory in others; *A Fair Quarrel* is a masterpiece, no doubt, but a decidedly imperfect masterpiece.

The later tragedies, written between 1611 and the end of Middleton's career, are not very different in this respect from the tragicomedies. At their best they illustrate the author's preoccupation with the minds of somewhat abnormal characters and his fondness for a kind of drama that can almost be called psychological, but at their worst they show his perverse indifference to the characters he has created and his willingness to sacrifice them or at least blur their outlines for the sake of a sensational incident or a violent ending. The

[1] M. C. Bradbrook, *Themes and Conventions of Elizabethan Tragedy* (Cambridge, 1935), p. 213.

virginity test and the final scene in *The Changeling* are examples, the latter indeed a scene that Middleton did not
actually write, but one that he presumably helped to plan.
It has been said that he was still too much under the influence of Beaumont and Fletcher, as no doubt he was, but one
feels that he would occasionally have lapsed into sensational-
ism even if Beaumont and Fletcher had never written, for
he was working within a dramatic tradition that was essentially alien to his genius. He was trying to transform the
melodramatic tragedy of his age into something like psychological tragedy, and he was not sufficiently sure of himself—
or his audience—to make the transformation complete. Hence
the faults that mar all his tragedies except perhaps *Women
Beware Women;* hence the tendency of his critics to regard
him as an author who was capable of writing great scenes but
not great plays.

I

The Second Maiden's Tragedy survives in a manuscript
prepared by a contemporary scribe and submitted to Sir
George Buc for licensing. The manuscript is annotated in
several hands—one presumably Buc's, one the prompter's,
and one that of a person who has been described as "the literary Corrector, almost certainly the author." [2] This last hand
does not seem to be Middleton's, but the style of the play
is so obviously his and the parallels with his acknowledged
work are so striking that there cannot really be much doubt
about the authorship. If any anonymous Jacobean play can
be ascribed to an author with almost absolute certainty on
internal evidence alone, then this one can.

Perhaps the most obvious thing to say about *The Second
Maiden's Tragedy* is that there is considerable disparity between the drama, which is generally second rate and pretty

[2] *The Second Maiden's Tragedy 1611,* ed. W. W. Greg, Malone Society
Reprints (Oxford, 1909), p. 1.

much what I have described above as Middleton at his worst,
and the style, which is always accomplished and sometimes
quite masterly. It is not—if I may begin at this point—quite
like the style of *The Revenger's Tragedy*, but more urbane,
more conversational, and more elusive. It relies for its characteristic effects as often as not on suggestion and association.
The vocabulary is somewhat abstract and the imagery somewhat difficult to visualize.

> wellcome to myne eyes
> as is the daye-springe from the morninges woombe—

presumably a favorite image of Middleton's since he used it
again two years later in *The Triumphs of Truth*—is a typical
example. There is a picture of a sort no doubt, but it is scarcely
one drawn from actual observation and is, in any case, suggested rather than completely realized. On the other hand,
the author is quite capable of surprising us from time to time
with homely, detailed, realistic images, clearly the result of
personal observation. There is the great city pie, gutted of its
meat before the crust is broken; and there is the woman on
the point of moving:

> I am like one
> removing from her howse, that lockes vp all
> and rather then she would displace her goodes
> makes shifte wth any thinge for the tyme shee staies.
>
> Lines 1321–24

Several times imagery is used to epitomize the tragic predica-
ment of the characters, and in the case of Anselmus, who is
not satisfied until he has subjected his wife to temptation, the
result is wonderfully detailed and precise. He is compared
first to a man who smashes a diamond and then to a man who
ruins a valuable watch.

> must a man needes in having a ritch Diamond
> put it betweene a hammer and an Anvile
> and not beleeving the true worth and valiew

breake it in pieces to finde owt the goodnes
and in the findinge loose it.   Lines 315–19

but he must haue her tride forsooth, and tempted
and when she proues a Queane then he lies quiet,
like one that has a watche of curious makinge,
thinckinge to be more cvnyñge then the workeman
neuer giues ouer tampringe wth the wheeles
till either springe be weakned, ballance bowde
or some wrong pin put in, and so spoiles all.   Lines 830–36

The domestic story of Anselmus and his wife—or the first
half of it at least—is easily the best part of the play. It is not
quite like anything in *The Revenger's Tragedy*, for Middleton's manner had profoundly changed in the meantime, but
very close to such plays as *More Dissemblers Besides Women*
and *The Changeling*. The characters are entirely human and
indeed interesting for their own sakes. They have inner lives
and the retribution that overtakes them is often mental as
well as physical. Anselmus—as the images above so perfectly
suggest—is a man who insists on ruining himself and who,
in fact, is never more satisfied with his marriage than at the
very moment his wife deceives him.

o when a mans opynion is at peace
tis a fine life to marrie; no states like it,

he says. Such is Leantio's reaction in *Women Beware Women*
at the very moment *his* wife deceives *him*, and such indeed
is the very language he uses.

How near am I now to a happiness
That earth exceeds not! not another like it.   III.i.82–83

Votarius, the Wife's lover, struggles with his lust, much as
Leantio struggles later, but he soon gives in to it altogether
and experiences inevitable jealousy. "My very thought's my
poison," he says, and it proves a potent poison indeed. The
Wife herself is the victim of her servant, Leonela, much as

Beatrice-Joanna in *The Changeling* is the victim of De Flores. She is blind, and her servant, who is remarkably clear-sighted, eggs her on, realizing the advantages she stands to gain. So in the act of betraying her husband, the Wife betrays herself—puts herself in her servant's power and completely relinquishes control of her own destiny.

The tragedy is like the tragedy of *A Fair Quarrel* in that it is over long before the final scene. The characters have for the most part faced the consequences of their sin and fully realized what they have done to themselves; there is no need for more. But just as in *A Fair Quarrel*, Middleton insists on going on and providing, not indeed a happy ending in this case, but a great deal of gratuitous slaughter. He has his characters plot and counter-plot, clash with swords in their hands and stab one another until no one is left alive to carry the dead bodies from the stage. He has apparently forgotten the real tragedy of the play in his desire for violence and death.

The other—the principal—story in *The Second Maiden's Tragedy* is less satisfactory at the beginning and even more melodramatic at the end. For if Middleton again shows some signs of trying to humanize his characters, it can scarcely be said that he gets very far with the main ones. The Tyrant is closer to the inflated tyrants of Fletcher than to the superficially similar character of Vortiger in Middleton's *Hengist*; the Lady is just a very chaste lady and Govianus is just a hero. As elsewhere in his later drama, Middleton shows a tendency to work over incidents from *The Revenger's Tragedy*. A father, for example, conveys dishonorable proposals to his daughter until a pistol shot awakens his better instincts; a villain kisses a dead woman whose lips have been anointed with poison. But no effort is made to recapture the mood of the earlier play or indeed to create any mood at all. The melodrama is in this case mere melodrama, never really helping the author to describe court life or to express a view of human nature.

II

It can perhaps be said that Middleton's tragedies are like those of Shakespeare in that they are all more or less experimental. He tries something new in every one of them, and whether he succeeds or fails he never exactly repeats himself in a subsequent play or shows any tendency to reduce his work to a formula. In *The Second Maiden's Tragedy* he combines domestic drama with the older sort of court intrigue, obviously with imperfect success, but instead of trying the same thing again with different stories and a different technique, he abandons it altogether. In *Hengist, King of Kent*—or *The Mayor of Quinborough,* as it is called in the quarto—he turns to an old form, by this time distinctly antiquated, the chronicle play. Now one of the distinguishing marks of the chronicle is that it is so very episodic; the author, setting out to dramatize a period in history or a king's reign, feels free to put in almost anything he wants to. In *Hengist* Middleton permits himself this freedom. If he follows in a general way the career of the early British usurper Vortiger, he offers us, at one time or another, epic or something like it, a study of sainthood, buffoonery of the most primitive sort, and more court intrigue.

The epic story, concerned with the Saxon invasion of Britain, is presumably one that would have interested the early dramatists who wrote chronicle plays, but in Middleton it gets only the most cursory attention. There are some remarks by the presenter, along with a dumb show, at the beginning— for the author is unwilling to spare us the naïveté of the older drama—two scenes in the middle, and a few lines at the end. The upshot of it is that the Saxon invasion fails and so perhaps the story cannot really be called epic after all. The study of sainthood is equally brief but far more impressive. Constantius, delineated in two scenes, is one of the really memorable characters in Middleton's later drama.

Sainthood may not seem to fall within Middleton's province, but actually there are saints of one sort or another in several of his plays. There is the Lady in *The Second Maiden's Tragedy*, for example, and there is Castiza in *The Revenger's Tragedy* itself. But Constantius is not very closely related to either of these characters or to the saints in medieval mystery plays or to those parlor saints in T. S. Eliot who, when they leave the world, set out on such genteel journeys. For Constantius is first of all a human being, a portrait of a saint by a great realist, not entirely different—if such a comparison is possible—from another saint, the Master of Santiago, drawn by another great realist, Henry de Montherlant. Pronounced by his father as "vnfitt for gouerment and rule" and therefore forced into a monastery, Constantius has become so devout and so completely preoccupied with the routine of devotion that contacts with the outer world are painful to him. Nevertheless he is too weak to refuse such contacts when they are pressed upon him by the Machiavellian Vortiger, and so he becomes king and so he suffers, one after another, the various vexations of kingship, protesting all the time, incompetent, opinionated, somewhat priggish, but wonderfully eloquent. A note of sustained querulousness is seldom absent from his speeches.

> Pray doe not follow me, vnles you doot
> To wonder at my garm[en]ts: theirs noe Cause
> I giue you why you shold: tis shame enough
> Me thinks for me to looke vpon my selfe;
> It greiues me that more shold: the other weeds
> Became me better; but ye Lordes are pleasd
> To force mee to weare these, I would not els:
> I pray be satisfied, I Calld you not.

Wonder of madness! can you stand soe Idle
And know that you must dye.   I.ii.48–57

He is never more the saint than when he stays away from
dinner on Saint Agatha's Eve. "I neuer eate on Eues," he
says. But since he is an imperfect saint, he yields to pressure
and goes in to dinner after all.

Constantius eludes martyrdom only until the beginning of
the second act and thereafter the play drifts off into a different sort of drama and one closer to the early Middleton.
Vortiger is infatuated with Roxena, and to get her is prepared
to ruin his queen, the saintly Castiza. With the usual per-
versity displayed by Middleton characters, he turns for help
to the very man he should avoid—Horsus, Roxena's lover.
"Oh faithfull treasure,/" he says to Horsus. "All my lost happiness is made vp in thee." But he is no sooner out of earshot
than Horsus scoffs: "Ile follow you through ye world, to
Cuckold you/ Thats my way now." The situation comes from
The Revenger's Tragedy, where it is used with several vari-
ants, and the ending comes from that play too. Roxena's infidelity is revealed to Vortiger in his last moments much as
the Duchess's is revealed to the Duke, and indeed much as
the Wife's in *The Second Maiden's Tragedy* is revealed to
Anselmus.

The characters in this part of the play generally lack depth
and distinction, but Horsus is an exception and a very notable
one. At first he shows strong neurotic tendencies in that his
jealousy of Roxena affects him in a quite physical way. He
feels "a paine like a Convulsion/ A Crampe at hart," and
afterwards falls down in what might be, and what is indeed
represented to the onlookers as, an epileptic fit. Ostensibly
he is somewhat of a weakling, yet as the play goes on no one
turns out to be stronger. When he is invited to ruin Castiza,
he shows such remarkable knowledge of underworld trickery
and such remarkable competence in carrying it out that even

Vortiger is amazed. "I admire him," Vortiger exclaims, as though involuntarily. The ruling passion of Horsus is no doubt lust for Roxena—it is, after all, for her sake that he gives up his ambition and attaches himself to Vortiger—and yet his passion is so completely transformed by his intelligence that it scarcely seems to be lust at all. His vision is so wonderfully clear that he has no illusions of any kind, least of all about his mistress, whom he is always able to see quite dispassionately as she really is. "Tis her Cuning," he explains when she follows him from Germany,

> The loue of her owne lust, w[hi]ch makes a woman
> Gallop downe hill as feareless as a drunkard.   II.iii.189–91

He is able to appreciate the irony of her marriage to Vortiger and even able to laugh on the wedding night.

> Me thinks I should not here from fortune next
> Vnder an Earledome now, she Cannot spend
> A night so Idely, but to make a Lord
> W[i]th ease, me thinks & play.   IV.ii.280–83

He is seen at his best in his asides, where he has full freedom to scoff at the illusions of others and where, once at least, he represents himself as a kind of destructive force in the world.

> euery one has his toye
> While he liues here: some men delight in Building,
> A tricke of Babell & will nere be left,
> Some in Consuming what was raysed w[i]th toyleing
> *Hengist* in getting honor, I in spoyleing.   IV.iii.160–64

Horsus is indeed a complex character—a strange mixture of cruelty and affection, cynicism and lust. He is sometimes reminiscent of Webster's Flamineo but more often of Middleton's other study in lust—De Flores in *The Changeling*.

The buffoonery that accompanies and interrupts the serious action is occasionally related to the principal themes of the play. Simon, the clown—the chief comic character and the

one who becomes Mayor of Quinborough—has a rival in a
fustian-weaver named Oliver. Thus the political intrigue in
the story of Vortiger is echoed in farce. Once Simon threatens
to revive or torment Oliver if he faints by pouring aquavitae
down his throat; Horsus has actually done this to Castiza,
though he seems to have used, not aquavitae, but some even
more potent stimulant. (It is remarkable what a passion Middleton's characters have for keeping each other conscious. In
The Revenger's Tragedy Vindice will not let the Duke so
much as wink without threatening to tear up his eyelids.)
But on the whole the buffoonery must be condemned as mere
comic relief, indefensible in so serious a play, but still remarkably well done if considered apart from its context. It
shows Middleton in one of his rare moods of pure gaiety—
not easily illustrated elsewhere in his work except perhaps in
Anything for a Quiet Life—where he is not concerned with
human nature or with human life at all but quite content for
the time being with the wonderfully fantastic arabesques of
his plot. There is considerable variety in it, but the best scene
of all is certainly the one in which Simon entertains the actors. He is a clown himself and so he praises clowns, then
reprimands the clown in the play-within-the-play, then finally
takes over his part. Thus the two actions, the play and the
play-within-the-play, intertwine like something in expression-
istic drama, say an episode in *Six Characters in Search of an
Author*. The complexity of the comic effect is particularly
pleasing.

Hengist has faults which are only too obvious. Its quality
is uneven; it has scenes of great brilliance like those devoted
to Constantius in the first act, and scenes that are purely
perfunctory like those devoted to Castiza in the third and
fourth. It has, furthermore, the scenes of Simon which—
though extremely entertaining in themselves—are far too
genial for so sombre a play. And yet at its best it has a dark

grandeur that is not easy to parallel elsewhere in Middleton's serious work, not even in *The Changeling* and *Women Beware Women.*

III

If *Hengist* is a sophisticated chronicle play, *The Changeling* can perhaps be described as a play about a murder case— not a real case, since its source turns out to be fiction, but rather like a real one. The characters are by no means shopkeepers, but they live so far from courts and concern themselves so exclusively with their own private problems that their story can almost be classified as domestic. Interspersed among the episodes of this story are comic scenes, laid in an insane asylum, in which the chief character is a clown. Thus the play, though quite different from *Hengist,* involves a somewhat similar contrast of moods, and since it was written in collaboration it involves a further contrast—inadvertent in this case no doubt—of styles and points of view.

The murder story is set in motion by Rowley, who tells it in the amiable, vulgar, and conventional way that is so very characteristic of him. Alsemero and Beatrice-Joanna meet in church and promptly fall in love. Alsemero is portrayed as a young man with a passion for traveling and an allergy to cherries. Up to this time he has shown himself strangely indifferent to women, including the ones whom his mother, presumably somewhat alarmed, has paraded before him. Beatrice-Joanna regrets that she has just committed herself to marry another man, Alonzo de Piracquo. "For five days past," she exclaims,

> To be recall'd! sure mine eyes were mistaken;
> This was the man was meant for me: that he should come
> So near his time, and miss it!   I.i.85–88

Aside from loving Alsemero and being indifferent to Piracquo, she hates De Flores, still another of her admirers, who is described as "a gentleman/ In good respect with [her] father." Her hatred is very intense and entirely irrational since she can give no reason for it at all. Just at the end of the scene she refuses to accept a glove that De Flores has considerately picked up for her and indeed flings both her gloves down before him. De Flores is inclined to be grateful for what is after all a present of a sort and inclined to see its sex symbolism.

>   I know
> She had rather wear my pelt tann'd in a pair
> Of dancing pumps, than I should thrust my fingers
> Into her sockets here.   I.i.234–37

He goes on to say:

>   I know she hates me,
> Yet cannot choose but love her: no matter:
> *If but to vex her,* I will haunt her still.   I.i.237–39

I print five of his words in italics to show how absurdly conventional Rowley's motivation is.

In taking over the story at this point, Middleton not only gives it distinction, which so far it has completely lacked, but profoundly changes it in the process. For one thing, he all but eliminates the character of Alsemero, about whose passion for traveling and indifference to women we hear not a single word more. For Middleton is interested in Alsemero only as he influences Beatrice and henceforth we are permitted to see him only through her eyes. She tells us that he has *judgment*—the word is applied to him repeatedly, as the word *poison* is applied to De Flores [3]—but she is really throwing more light on herself than on him, indulging in self-deception, interpreting what is actually fickleness on her part as a kind of intellectual growth. "Methinks I love now

[3] Bradbrook, *Themes and Conventions of Elizabethan Tragedy*, pp. 214, 234.

with the eyes of judgment," she says. If the part played by
Alsemero is minimized, that of De Flores is changed. His
passion for the heroine is made fiercer and more physical so
that he could never conceivably say, as though he were involved in a parlor game, "If but to vex her, I will haunt her
still." Her hatred of him is no longer a mystery, for as
described by Middleton he is a really appalling creature with,
specifically, a hideously pimpled face. The most graphic passage about him ("he's so foul/ One would scarce touch [him]
with a sword he lov'd," etc.) comes much later in the play,
but even at this point we are never allowed to forget that,
physically at least, De Flores is a monster.

Having thus rescued his characters from Rowley, Middleton proceeds at once to a crucial episode. Beatrice is talking
with Alsemero, assuring him of her love and arguing that
he should not try to settle the issue with Piracquo by chal-
lenging him to a duel. He might himself be killed or thrown
in jail or forced to leave the country. "Here was a course,"
she says,

> Found to bring sorrow on her way to death;
> The tears would ne'er ha' dried, till dust had chok'd 'em.
> Blood-guiltiness becomes a fouler visage.   II.ii.37–40

A fouler visage! The words inevitably remind her of De
Flores and—in an aside—she at once determines to use him
as an instrument of murder.

>   the ugliest creature
> Creation fram'd for some use; yet to see
> I could not mark so much where it should be! . . .
> Why, men of art make much of poison,
> Keep one to expel another; where was my art?   II.ii.43–47

There is no hesitation, no mental struggle, no consideration
of consequences: the idea of murder no sooner occurs to her
than she accepts it. The modern reader, brought up on *Mac-*

beth, may feel that this is too sudden, but he can scarcely deny that it is deliberate. For Middleton is quite clearly illustrating his view, implicit in some of his other plays at least, that women seldom show much sense of morality or much inclination to expostulate with themselves. In *The Changeling* he is specifically concerned with a woman who has no sense of morality at all and who is so set on getting her "will" that she becomes completely irresponsible.

During its central scenes the play takes on that wonderful and terrible concentration that contributes so much to its effectiveness. The two characters, the willful girl and the monster, are alone on the stage much of the time, and in any case the drama is entirely concerned with the interaction of their personalities and the way in which, by appealing to each other's weaknesses, they realize their tragic destiny. It stands out in the history of English tragedy as one of the supreme examples of purely psychological interest. Of the two, De Flores is the more complex and so much like Horsus in Middleton's chronicle play that he may well have been drawn from the same model. At the beginning he too seems to be both neurotic and weak. He keeps inventing excuses to see Beatrice even though he knows that she will drive him away—

> I must see her still!
> I shall have a mad qualm within this hour again,
> I know't—

and he keeps trying, rather too hard it seems, to cheer himself up. "I must confess," he says,

> my face is bad enough,
> But I know far worse has better fortune,
> And not endur'd alone, but doted on.   II.i.37–39

> I'll despair the less,
> Because there's daily precedents of bad faces

Belov'd beyond all reason; these foul chops
May come into favour one day 'mongst their fellows:
Wrangling has prov'd the mistress of good pastime;
As children cry themselves asleep, I ha' seen
Women have chid themselves a-bed to men.   II.i.82–88

This looks like wishful thinking, but actually it is anything
but that. For De Flores resembles Horsus too in that he is a
man with a remarkably penetrating intelligence, who is seldom wrong either about himself or others. It is this rather
than his ugliness that makes him so terrifying in his en-
counters with the heroine.

I have said that Middleton's tragedies are all distinctly
different from one another, but I should not want to imply
that he avoids repeating himself or that he is in any way reluctant to use an episode or a character just because he has
used it before. The central episode in *The Changeling*—that
of the sinner who in the act of sin betrays himself to the
wrong person—is obviously a favorite of his. He has used it
in *The Revenger's Tragedy*, where both Lussurioso and the
Duke betray themselves to Vindice, and in the chronicle play,
where Vortiger betrays himself to Horsus. The sinner is always as blind as Beatrice, for in Middleton's view sin *is*
blindness—or "forgetfulness," as he seems to call it elsewhere—and the person who victimizes the sinner always
comes close to De Flores in intelligence. But in the example
before us the episode is handled with so much emphasis on
the interplay of character and so little on the theory of retribution that it really seems to be a new one after all. Beatrice
thinks that she is giving a consummate performance, as indeed she is. She touches the monster's pimples, decides that
they come from the heat of the liver, and promises—since
the author's irony is already in evidence—to make a wash
that will cure them in a fortnight. De Flores is certainly
aroused in a purely physical way, but he is not for a moment

taken in—his mind is still perfectly clear. " 'Tis the same physnomy," he says aside,

> to a hair and pimple,
> Which she call'd scurvy scarce an hour ago:
> How is this?   II.ii.76–78

He watches her closely as, encouraged by what she takes to be her success, she goes on with her performance, and he no sooner hears her hint that she has found him employment than he realizes how completely he has her at his mercy. There is irony even in the stage business, for he kneels at the very moment he comes to this realization.

During the rest of the scene Middleton underscores the irony by having his two characters talk at cross purposes. Beatrice is now so completely blind that she thinks De Flores is interested in money and she even offers him some. "There's to encourage thee," she says;

> As thou art forward, and thy service dangerous,
> Thy reward shall be precious.   II.ii.129–31

But De Flores, who has already foreseen everything, knows exactly what his reward is to be. "That I've thought on," he answers;

> I have assur'd myself of that beforehand,
> And know it will be precious; the thought ravishes!
>
> II.ii.131–33

She leaves, congratulating herself on getting rid of two "loathings at one time,/ Piracquo, and his dog-face," while he imagines, in a very precise way, how she will act when she is dependent on him for sexual pleasure—how she will comb out his beard with her wanton fingers and at the moment of enjoyment even praise his repulsive face. He goes on to say what he has twice said earlier, but how different it seems now when his desires are on the point of fulfillment!

> Hunger and pleasure, they'll commend sometimes
> Slovenly dishes, and feed heartily on 'em.
> Nay, which is stranger, refuse daintier for 'em:
> Some women are odd feeders.   II.ii.152–55

In the second of their great scenes together they continue to talk at cross purposes, Beatrice still so blind as to go on offering money and De Flores now openly insisting that he wants something quite different. Finally, when she cannot help understanding him, she tries to escape by pleading her modesty and then her noble birth, but he has the perfect answer to every plea.

> Push! fly not to your birth, but settle you
> In what the act has made you; you're no more now.
> You must forget your parentage to me;
> You are the deed's creature; by that name
> You lost your first condition, and I challenge you,
> As peace and innocency has turn'd you out,
> And made you one with me.   III.iv.135–41

"You are the deed's creature"—it is the most significant sentence in the play. Beatrice kneels, just as De Flores knelt earlier, but there is no irony now and for her no escape. De Flores is indeed reassuring as he raises her from the ground. "Thy peace is wrought for ever in this yielding," he says, and he means of course that he is offering her physical pleasure.

> 'Las! how the turtle pants! thou'lt love anon
> What thou so fear'st and faint'st to venture on.
>
>   III.iv.170–71

If his intelligence has a limitation it lies in the fact that he sees nothing in life beyond sex.

The tragedy is so nearly complete at this point—the end of the third act—that in the final acts Middleton is forced to do a good deal of improvising. He puts in something about an amateur detective, the irascible brother of the murdered Piracquo; something about a ghost (who first appears in dumb show!); and something, rather a good deal in fact, about a virginity test, a variant of an extended and distasteful episode in *Hengist*. The story is in danger of going to pieces long before Rowley gets his hands on it again, but some of it at least is relevant. A few touches here and there tell us, quite casually and as though incidentally, what we need to know about the two tragic figures whose lives have become so intimately intertwined. Beatrice is as ruthless as ever but apparently older and less confident. In a few lines Middleton skillfully portrays her desperation on the wedding night,

> I'm afraid now:
> This night hath been so tedious! O this strumpet!
> Had she a thousand lives, he should not leave her
> Till he had destroy'd the last. List! O my terrors!
>
> V.i.63–66

and in her anguished cry, "I must trust somebody," he suggests the isolation from which she inevitably suffers. Her crime, committed for the sake of Alsemero, has cut her off from Alsemero forever. She must trust someone, someone else—must, in fact, trust De Flores, the pimpled monster who has been her accomplice. De Flores has grown in stature in the course of the play. At first ostensibly a weakling, he develops into a really masterful figure who not only wins a mistress despite almost insuperable obstacles but afterwards protects her with a remarkable display of competence. In this he is exactly like Horsus, a fellow "good on all occasions," as one of the other characters remarks. "He hath a ready wit; he's worth 'em all, sir." And naturally enough it is his competence—and not his masculinity, as he supposed —that finally endears him to Beatrice. "I'm forc'd to love thee now," she exclaims as he swiftly outlines a plan to deal

with the lecherous Diaphanta, and when he has left the stage
she goes on to say:

> How heartily he serves me! his face loathes one;
> But look upon his care, who would not love him?
> The east is not more beauteous than his service.   V.i.69–71

She afterwards describes him as a man worth loving, and it is
perfectly clear that she does love him, that unconsciously her
feelings toward him have undergone a profound change. It
is the final or at least the final significant phase of her career.

The very last scene, written by Rowley, adds nothing to
the play but a little pointless violence, and the comic story,
also by Rowley, adds even less. It would be nice, in fact, if
we could forget that the play has a comic story at all, but the
critics will not permit this.[4] They assure us that there is a
subtle relationship between comic and tragic, that in planning
the play the collaborators were aiming at a higher unity. A
somewhat esoteric little literature has in fact grown up on the
subject. It is pointed out that the title applies to both stories.
Beatrice is a changeling because she changes her mind about
the man she wants to marry, and Antonio is a changeling in
the Jacobean sense (a child changed in the cradle) because
he is or pretends to be an idiot. So much is certainly true, but
when the critics add De Flores to their list—sometimes calling him the real changeling of the play—because he is repulsive and therefore another example of the fairy child, I am
inclined to think the reasoning somewhat fanciful. If change-
lings have to be multiplied, I should myself prefer to fix on
Alsemero, who at least changes brides on his wedding night.
It might also be pointed out that there is one genuine case of

---

[4] See William Empson, *Some Versions of Pastoral* (London, 1935), pp.
48–52; Bradbrook, *Themes and Conventions of Elizabethan Tragedy*,
pp. 213–24; Karl L. Holzknecht, "The Dramatic Structure of *The Changeling*," *Renaissance Papers*, 1954, pp. 77–87.

parallelism between the stories. Lollio, the clown, puts in for a "share" of Isabella when he suspects her of infidelity much as De Flores "puts in for one" with Beatrice when he over-hears her interview with Alsemero. But this scarcely carries us very far; there is nowhere a suggestion of parallelism that can be described as fundamental or significant. In any case, unity depends on the quality as well as the kind of com-ponents, and whatever the intentions of the authors, no real unity can be expected from a play in which the tragedy is as brilliant and the comedy as completely contemptible as in this one. Middleton does better with the combination in *Hengist*, where the comedy is at least good, and better still in *Women Beware Women*, where his method is entirely different.

The comedy, the inferior tragic scenes of Rowley at the beginning and the end, and the inferior scenes by Middleton himself in the fourth and fifth acts are all unfortunate weak-nesses in *The Changeling*, and I might add to the list still another weakness or at least a limitation. The dialogue is not quite so imaginative as in Middleton's other tragedies; there is less grandeur and less concern with the larger aspects of human destiny. No one, seeing a castle for the first time, is reminded of the Last Judgment,

> Methinks it looks as if it mockt all ruin
> Saue that greate M[aste]rpeece of Consum[m]ation,
> The end of time, w[hi]ch must Consume even ruin
> And eate that into Cinders,

and no one says,

> Theirs nothing makes man ffeele his miseries,
> But knowledge only.[5]

---

[5] *Hengist, King of Kent*, ed. R. C. Bald (New York and London, 1938), IV.ii.7–10 and I.i.157–58. Cf. *Women Beware Women*, III.ii.325–26:

> For nothing makes man's loss grievous to him
> But knowledge of the worth of what he loses.

The style here is barer, necessarily so since Middleton is concerned with domestic tragedy, barer and at the same time more highly concentrated. For concentration is in the end the quality that stands out in *The Changeling* and distinguishes it most clearly both in style and structure from Middleton's other tragedies. It tells a very simple story, in almost Ibsenesque language and in a remarkably short space—the greater part of it indeed in two scenes—about a willful girl who betrays herself into the hands of the man she loathes and then learns to love him.[6]

IV

Women Beware Women is so different in structure from *The Changeling* that it might almost have been planned by a different author. It is closer to *The White Devil* than to *The Duchess of Malfi,* closer to *The Broken Heart* than to *Perkin Warbeck:* it has no central figure. Leantio and Bianca are no doubt most important in the main plot, Isabella is most important in the underplot, but there is also the tremendous figure of Livia, who is important in both. The play is really a reversion to *The Revenger's Tragedy,* an example of the kind of drama in which several stories are told simultaneously and several characters—here at least four—are almost equally prominent. The characters, set side by side and all to some extent similar, seem to give us a picture, not so much of court life in this case—since the court is the setting only in certain scenes—as of human life in general.

Beatrice in *The Changeling* is a fairly simple character, lecherous no doubt, since she shows a strong incidental interest in wedding nights, but doomed primarily because her

---

[6] Symons speaks of the "bareness" and "fierce reticence" of the dialogue; "there is a restraint," he says, "never paralleled elsewhere in [Middleton's] work; nowhere else are words used with such fruitful frugality, or so much said in so little" (*Cambridge History of English Literature,* Cambridge, 1932, VI, 76).

sense of morality is defective. The characters in *Women Beware Women* are more complex. They are more definitely
moved by the passions of lust and greed, but they are also
more inclined to show twinges of conscience, evanescent, but
nevertheless distinct. Leantio, the most prominent character
at the beginning of the play, is another of Middleton's curled
darlings, a young man very much concerned with sex and—
since he is obliged to work hard for a precarious living—one
very much interested in money. When the play opens he has
already made his tragic mistake; he has stolen an heiress—the
notorious Bianca Capello of Italian history—and brought her
home to share his poverty. It is quite clear that his passion for
her is too completely physical, as he himself suggests when
he describes the place of sex in a well-ordered life.

> As fitting is a government in love
> As in a kingdom; where 'tis all mere lust,
> 'Tis like an insurrection in the people,
> That, rais'd in self-will, wars against all reason;
> But love that is respective for increase
> Is like a good king, that keeps all in peace.[7]   I.iii.43–48

Thus for a moment we see the stars from this pit of lechery,
and Leantio sees them too, for he struggles with himself
much as the heroes of Shakespeare struggle, except that in
their case the struggle emphasizes their nobility, in his, only
his weakness and lust. But what Middleton dwells on chiefly,
even in his choice of metaphor, is the economic aspect of
Leantio's mistake. He is guilty of theft, he has set in motion
economic forces of which he is as yet incompletely aware.
"You know not what you've done," his mother tells him.

> What ableness have you to do her right then
> In maintenance fitting her birth and virtues?

---

[7] Cf. *A Chaste Maid in Cheapside*, II.i.50–51:

> The feast of marriage is not lust, but love,
> And care of the estate.

Which every woman of necessity looks for,
And most to go above it, not confin'd
By their conditions, virtues, bloods, or births,
But flowing to affections, wills, and humours.   I.i.65–70

The generalization is ominous, but Leantio merely urges his mother to speak lower. Bianca has never revealed such desires and he will keep her contented by keeping her isolated from the world. She is his jewel—the image is persistently used— he will case her up in his house, and as for thieves,

Who could imagine now a gem were kept
Of that great value under this plain roof?   I.i.171–72

It is inevitable in Middleton that even-handed justice should manifest itself and that Leantio should experience retribution exactly proportioned to his crime. He has been guilty of theft and so must suffer from theft in turn; he must lose Bianca in the very way he has won her. When the second theft occurs, his grief seems genuine enough and at times he comes close to being a sympathetic figure. Once—in a kind of passage rare in Middleton, a glimpse into the past—he remembers nostalgically the days of his courtship.

Canst thou forget
The dear pains my love took? how it has watch'd
Whole nights together, in all weathers, for thee,
Yet stood in heart more merry than the tempest
That sung about mine ears,—like dangerous flatterers,
That can set all their mischief to sweet tunes,—
And then receiv'd thee, from thy father's window,
Into these arms at midnight: when we embrac'd
As if we had been statues only made for't,
To shew art's life, so silent were our comforts,
And kiss'd as if our lips had grown together?   III.ii.252–62

And once, in an entirely different mood, he threatens Bianca magnificently.

> I shall find time
> To play a hot religious bout with some of you,
> And, perhaps, drive you and your course of sins
> To their eternal kennels. I speak softly now. . .
> But come I to your everlasting parting once,
> Thunder shall seem soft music to that tempest.   IV.i.83–90

But at crucial points in the story he is so mean as to be utterly contemptible. He accepts a favor, the captainship of the fort, from the Duke, who has taken Bianca, and he accepts money to become an older woman's lover—not only accepts it but buys a new suit and hurries off to Bianca's lodging to flaunt his finery in her face. Husband and wife—now stallion and whore—meet on almost equal terms, but Leantio, always the weaker of the two, is the first to break down. "You're a whore," he screams.

> *Bianca.* Fear nothing, sir.
> *Leantio.* An impudent, spiteful strumpet!
> *Bianca.* O, sir, you give me thanks for your captainship!
>   I thought you had forgot all your good manners.
>   IV.i.62–65

Bianca, Leantio's companion in this sordid scene, is more difficult to analyze because she seems different at different times. It is perhaps possible to say that she is treated like one of Proust's characters. Nearly every time she appears we get a fresh impression of her, somewhat different from the last one; we are aware that she has changed in the interval, but we cannot be sure just why. It seems apparent that Middleton is trying to telescope into five acts a development that in real life covered a period of years and one that struck him as unusually complicated.[8]

Glimpses into the past, permitted by Middleton in Bianca's

---

[8] See Empson, *Some Versions of Pastoral*, p. 55: ". . . she is first the poor man's modest wife, then the Duke's grandiose and ruthless mistress; the idea of 'development' is irrelevant to her."

case too, show us that she has always been aggressive—good at wrangling for what she wants, as she puts it—and that her upbringing has been somewhat too strict. "Restraint," she herself says,

> Breeds wandering thoughts, as many fasting days
> A great desire to see flesh stirring again:
> I'll ne'er use any girl of mine so strictly.   IV.i.32–35

But these are detached observations, not very clearly related to the other things we know about her. In the first scene she is certainly anything but aggressive since she stands on the stage for something like 125 lines without speaking so much as a single word. Presumably the boy who acted the part made some suggestions about her character in pantomime, but none of this survives in stage directions. When she finally does speak, in this scene and in her next one, she shows that her passion for Leantio is even more completely physical than his for her. She is preoccupied with kisses and nights—and not only wedding nights like the heroine of *The Changeling*. Otherwise, her conversation, not very easy to interpret, may indicate good nature or a careful education or hypocrisy or just naïveté. In her third scene, she falls into adultery, not, however, without a brief struggle. She appeals to "religion" and speaks of sexual sin as death,

> Make me not bold with death and deeds of ruin,
> Because they fear not you,

much as the Cardinal, the moralist of the play, does later. The Duke threatens to use force and then addresses himself to her mercenary instincts.

> Do not I know you've cast away your life
> Upon necessities, means merely doubtful
> To keep you in indifferent health and fashion—
> A thing I heard too lately, and soon pitied—
> And can you be so much your beauty's enemy,

> To kiss away a month or two in wedlock,
> And weep whole years in wants for ever after?
> Come, play the wise wench, and provide for ever.
>
> II.ii.380–87

Stage directions are again lacking and so it is not quite clear how Bianca reacts to this, but it is at least possible that she is won over. If so, Middleton is again underscoring economic motivation and illustrating what Livia says in a later scene.

> Young gentlemen that only love for beauty,
> They love not wisely; such a marriage rather
> Proves the destruction of affection;
> It brings on want, and want's the key of whoredom.
>
> III.ii.282–85

Seduction brings with it a good deal of sophistication in Bianca's speech and a good deal of the aggressiveness she is said to have shown in her childhood. She blasts Guardiano with invective and irony, she crushes Livia with a really devastating aside, and once she is at home again, she is persistently querulous, demanding luxury of one sort or another and indeed acting exactly as Leantio's mother hinted she would. It is quite clear that, by this time at least, her motive is greed or ambition or pride, as it is sometimes called. Leantio is certainly wrong in accusing her of lust, since the disparity between her age and the Duke's—one is specified as sixteen and the other as fifty-five—seems to preclude a strong physical attachment on her part. On the other hand, she is particularly brazen in sin, as Leantio complains, and very much the "glistering whore." During the last part of the play we are shown various aspects of her new personality—her wit, her intelligence, her cynicism, her eloquence, and her effrontery. These qualities and especially the last ones—so magnificently illustrated in her address to the Cardinal—give her at times a strong resemblance to another "glorious dangerous strumpet" of Renaissance Italy, Vittoria Corombona. She dies—it is one of those fanciful touches that Middleton can so seldom resist—after she has kissed poison from the lips of the Duke. The incident, vaguely reminiscent of *The Revenger's Tragedy*, comes close here to having symbolic force, like the death by fire of Roxena in *Hengist* and Diaphanta in *The Changeling*.

The third tragic character, Isabella, is less frequently on the stage than Bianca, but in one or two scenes at the beginning of the play she is almost as distinctly realized. She is being forced by her father to marry the simple-minded Ward, and she resists with real dignity, not only because she loathes the Ward—"more than beauty can hate death,/ Or age her spiteful neighbour"—but because she loves her uncle Hippolito. She and Hippolito are always together, day and night, spinning out hour after hour in aimless conversation. But Isabella is not aware that her love is partly physical, and when Hippolito points it out to her by confessing his own desire, her reaction is as conventional as Bianca's first reaction to the Duke. She will simply never see Hippolito again.

> What's become
> Of truth in love, if such we cannot trust,
> When blood, that should be love, is mix'd with lust?
>
> I.ii.229–31

Actually, however, her passion seems to become stronger by becoming more articulate, and in any case very little is needed to make her yield. That little is supplied by the bawd Livia, who lies to her—persuades her that she is an illegitimate child, that Hippolito is not her uncle, and that she will not really be guilty of incest if she gives herself to him. She goes to him, scarcely able to control her feelings. "Prithee, forgive me," she begins,

> I did but chide in jest; the best loves use it
> Sometimes, it sets an edge upon affection:
> When we invite our best friends to a feast,

> 'Tis not all sweetmeats that we set before them;
> There's somewhat sharp and salt, both to whet appetite
> And make 'em taste their wine well; so, methinks,
> After a friendly, sharp, and savoury chiding,
> A kiss tastes wondrous well, and full o' the grape.
>
> II.i.195–203

She kisses him and we are reminded of Bianca's lecherous kisses a scene or two before. But, unlike Bianca, she has very little to do in the rest of the play. She can only discover that her sin is incest after all, can only vow revenge against Livia, and to accomplish it take part in the patterned intrigue of the final act.

Hippolito is a rather conventional figure, colorless early in the play and inconsistent later, but Livia is magnificent throughout, fully deserving her reputation as one of Middleton's most memorable characters. Her social position is not perhaps as clear as it might be, but she certainly does pimping for her betters, her reward being "wealth and favour" at court. She seems to have—if a mere student of literature may form an opinion on such a matter—many of the qualities that make for successful pimping. She is ostensibly amiable, supremely clever, and completely unscrupulous. Furthermore, she has a strong sense of her own artistry.

> Sir, I could give as shrewd a lift to chastity
> As any she that wears a tongue in Florence;
> Sh'ad need be a good horsewoman, and sit fast,
> Whom my strong argument could not fling at last.
>
> II.i.36–39

It has recently been suggested that she has an incestuous passion for her brother Hippolito,[9] but this seems rather like gilding the lily and, furthermore, involves attributing an

[9] Daniel Dodson, "Middleton's Livia," *Philological Quarterly*, XXVII (October, 1948), 376–81.

artistic error to Middleton, who would not normally set three cases of incest side by side. Still, Livia is certainly very fond of her brother and quite willing for his sake to display her art gratis, even though she is a little querulous about it afterwards.

> I take a course to pity him so much now,
> That I've none left for modesty and myself.
> This 'tis to grow so liberal: you've few sisters
> That love their brothers' ease 'bove their own honesties;
> But if you question my affections,
> That will be found my fault.   II.i.68–73

What she does for Hippolito, however, is merely preliminary to what she does for the Duke, when substantial rewards are at stake. The scene is one of the finest in the whole of Jacobean drama, and Livia's performance one of the most astonishing. For, working as though by instinct and forming a perfect team with Guardiano, she does everything right— hits on exactly the right blandishments and plays on exactly the right weaknesses. Her artistry is so wonderful and her domination so complete that the whole scene can almost be described as a reflection of her personality. The famous irony of the chess game is to a large extent her irony and the wit her wit.

Middleton's morality is, however, inexorable, and this scene is necessarily followed by a companion scene in which, like the other characters, Livia is hoist with her own petard. She has betrayed two women to lust, and so she is herself betrayed by the same passion. The instrument is no other than Leantio. Having once set eyes on him, she dotes on him hopelessly. "I am not yet so old but he may think of me," she says, and she seems entirely human now. She goes on to say— it is a particularly human touch—that she is going to take up cosmetics again.

But I'll begin the week, and paint to-morrow,
So follow my true labour day by day;
I never thriv'd so well as when I us'd it.   III.ii.140–42

While Leantio whines about the loss of Bianca, Livia hovers near him, well aware that she is doing the wrong thing and that, at the very moment she needs it most, her artistry has deserted her completely.

'Tis as unseasonable to tempt him now
So soon, as [for] a widow to be courted
Following her husband's corse, or to make bargain
By the grave-side, and take a young man there.

          III.ii.314–17

Still she goes on blundering, she cannot control herself. Nor can she control herself later when Leantio lies dead at her feet, killed by the brother she loved so much. As the inexperienced Bianca becomes the glistering whore of the later scenes, so here a masterful middle-aged woman is finally presented as an example of lechery and incompetence.

It can perhaps be said that *Women Beware Women* is a more sordid play than *Hengist* or *The Changeling* since, in addition to lust, which is even more heavily underscored in it, there is a good deal about the meaner passion of greed. Three of the four characters described above show an interest in money of one sort or another. In this respect, the play is similar to Middleton's city comedies, in which greed and lust, the desire for money and the desire for mutton, invariably go hand in hand. It is also similar of course to modern naturalistic drama, in which the same basic view of human nature is often presented. We are again reminded of the fact that Middleton is in some respects a transitional figure, close to Shakespeare and Webster—here the Shakespeare of *Timon* and the Webster of *The White Devil*—but almost equally close to the disciples of Zola.

The play is close to modern drama in another respect too. It is really a tragicomedy, not indeed one of the sort defined by Fletcher in *The Faithful Shepherdess* and exemplified in *Philaster*, but one like *The Cherry Orchard* or Giraudoux's *Electra*. It is a play in which serious and comic action are set side by side in an attempt to represent the variety and the multiplicity of life. But even this description of it is too rigid because actually there are quite different kinds of serious action and different kinds of comedy. The characters of the play might well be arranged in a descending scale, with Isabella and the Cardinal, who are always serious, at the top, with Bianca and Livia, whose wit at least is comic, a little lower down, with the Mother and Fabricio, two examples of comic stupidity, somewhat below the middle, and the Ward, who is always grossly farcical, at the bottom. These characters are often introduced together in the same scene so that significant contrasts—the contrapuntal effects so common in modern plays and novels—can be worked out. The mood of individual passages is constantly changing, yet there is scarcely a suggestion of what is offensively called comic relief, the specialty of Middleton's collaborator, Rowley. The play is enriched and not disrupted by the variety of its moods. A particularly fine example is the second scene in the third act, where the Duke ceremoniously pays court to Bianca and she shows off her cynical wit, where Leantio suffers and Livia dotes, where Fabricio goes into ridiculous explanations and the Ward makes vulgar sex jokes. Isabella sings and dances— for there are ballet effects too—and the Ward even does a grotesque dance, a parody of a performance by Hippolito. Having begun with the vulgarities of the Ward and afterwards touched on nearly all the chief themes of the play, the scene finally comes to an end with the surrender of Leantio and the lecherous kiss that Livia gives him. To find anything nearly so contrapuntal in English drama we must turn to the wonderfully clever second act in *The Plough and the Stars*.

I have perhaps suggested that the play is wholly realistic or naturalistic, but this is not quite the case—or at least there are certain exceptional scenes and passages. One of them is the famous chess scene in the second act. Lamb says that it "has the air of being an immediate transcript from life," [10] as no doubt from certain points of view it does. The Mother might be anyone's next-door neighbor, and the other characters all act with exemplary realism. The trick on which the scene turns is one that the masterful Livia might naturally think up. Yet when all this is said, something remains, an element of ingenuity, a tendency on the part of the author to impose personal patterns on his drama, that is not quite realistic. The chess scene is, after all, not many steps removed from *A Game at Chess*. Another example of somewhat the same sort of thing is the passage, apparently imitated from Dekker, in which Bianca and the members of her retinue use the language of clocks.

> *Bianca*. How goes your watches, ladies? what's a'clock now?
> *First Lady*. By mine, full nine.
> *Second Lady*. By mine, a quarter past.
> *First Lady*. I set mine by St. Mark's.
> *Second Lady*. St. Anthony's, they say,
>   Goes truer. . . .
> *Bianca*. I'll end this strife straight: I set mine by the sun;
>   I love to set by the best, one shall not then
>   Be troubled to set often.
> *Second Lady*. You do wisely in't.
> *Bianca*. If I should set my watch, as some girls do,
>   By every clock i' the town, 'twould ne'er go true;
>   And too much turning of the dial's point,
>   Or tampering with the spring, might in small time
>   Spoil the whole work too.   IV.i.1–15

[10] Lamb, *Specimens of English Dramatic Poets* (London, 1835), I, 167, note.

This is a Jacobean conceit and not realistic dialogue at all.
Still another example is the scene, imitated from Marston
this time, in which Leantio is given two contrasting soliloquies
on marriage, the first beginning with the lines,

> How near am I to a happiness
> That earth exceeds not! not another like it:
> The treasures of the deep are not so precious
> As are the conceal'd comforts of a man
> Lock'd up in woman's love,

and the second with,

> O thou, the ripe time of man's misery, wedlock,
> When all his thoughts, like overladen trees,
> Crack with the fruits they bear, in cares, in jealousies!
>
> III.i.271–73

These passages, all occurring in the first four acts of the
play, are, as I save said, exceptional, but in the fifth act the
exception becomes the rule and Middleton turns to something quite different. His endings in at least two of the tragedies written after *The Revenger's Tragedy* are unsatisfactory because the retribution he is concerned with is essentially
psychological—as in Beatrice's increasing dependence on De
Flores—and the slaughter he feels obliged to add to it
seems completely gratuitous. The ending of *Women Beware
Women* is another example, or would be if Middleton had
not brilliantly reverted to *The Revenger's Tragedy* in his
final scene, as he reverts to it in his structure.[11] The slaughter
is again embedded in pageantry and dancing; the theory of
retribution, already illustrated psychologically in the play
proper, is now given a series of fantastic embellishments.
Drama yields to something like ballet with distinct overtones
of symbolism. When the court has gathered on the upper
stage, figures as fanciful as those in Middleton's mayoralty

[11] There is also the similar but less successful ending in *Your Five
Gallants.*

shows appear—Hymen in a yellow robe, Ganymede in a blue robe powdered with stars, and Hebe in a white robe with golden stars. The figures, all carrying covered cups, dance a short dance, make obeisance, and then present their cups to the proper persons. "This," Bianca says, "is some antimasque belike." In the masque proper Isabella is "a Nymph, dressed with flowers and garlands, carrying a censer with fire in it," and the bawd Livia is, ironically, the marriage goddess Juno. The slaughter, once it begins, is quite indiscriminate and completely unrealistic. Isabella and Livia murder each other, one making use of poisoned fumes from the censer, at almost exactly the same moment. Guardiano arranges to kill Hippolito by means of a trap door and a hideous instrument called a caltrop, but there is a mistake and Guardiano is his own victim. Bianca prepares poison for her enemy the Cardinal, but again there is a mistake and the Duke drops dead. Bianca herself dies almost symbolically, as I have said, and so does Hippolito, who is shot with the poisoned arrows of cupids.

These fantastic developments—rather closer to *Midsummer Night's Dream* than to *King Lear*—help to make the play less sordid than it might otherwise be, and the poetry helps too. For *Women Beware Women* is poetically a very brilliant example of Middleton's genius, though not in this respect exactly like his other plays. The texture of the dialogue is richer; there is more aphorism and more imagery. It is as though Middleton, in this one case, had tried to cultivate the more ornate, more florid style of Webster. There are no doubt many passages that seem altogether characteristic of Middleton, many of those vague, elusive images so successfully used in his earlier works.

                              would a silence,
    As great as that which keeps among the graves,
    Had everlastingly chain'd up her tongue!   IV.ii.153–55

But there are also many images that are quite definite and precise, that seem to come directly from his observation. Preferment that springs from lust reminds him that gardeners' crops shoot up quickly in the rottenest grounds,

Even like a salad growing upon a dunghill.   III.ii.51

Leantio, who gets a sinecure just at the moment that he loses his wife, reminds him of a fellow

That eats his meat with a good appetite,
And wears a plague-sore that would fright a country.

III.ii.54–55

Hippolito's sense of honor, the touchiness of an ulcerous reputation, reminds him that "sores are vex'd with flies." This cannot quite be called a new aspect of his style since illustrations of it can be found elsewhere in his work—I have myself singled some out from *The Second Maiden's Tragedy*—but it is an aspect not so copiously or on the whole so brilliantly illustrated elsewhere. In this one play, written toward the end of his career, he has drawn on all his stylistic resources at once, and this seems fitting. For though *Women Beware Women* is not so well known as *The Changeling*, which is persistently chosen for anthologies, it is as a whole a far more perfect specimen of Middleton's art and deserves to rank as the masterpiece of his later years.

CHAPTER VIII

A Game at Chess and Conclusion

MIDDLETON'S last play, *A Game at Chess*, is so different from his tragedies and tragicomedies that it demands treatment in a separate chapter. It is the product of his interest in politics, which was possibly stimulated after 1620 by his work as Chronologer to the City of London; it expresses the popular anti-Catholic and anti-Spanish feeling that became particularly intense in London after 1623, when Prince Charles returned from Madrid without his Spanish bride.

The historical events on which the play is based have often been described. King James was interested—had, in fact, been interested for a long time—in a Spanish marriage for his son. He wanted to reconcile the greatest Catholic and the greatest Protestant powers of Europe and to bring about an era of international peace. He received encouragement from the Spanish Ambassador, Count Gondomar, an able diplomat and an entertaining companion, and it was, in fact, through the efforts of Gondomar that the journey of Prince Charles to Madrid was ultimately arranged. But the negotiations failed, the Prince returned, and the City of London, at last sure that a Spaniard would not share the English throne, welcomed him with tumultuous joy. Bonfires blazed and feasting went on in the streets; bells rang and "Ordnance thundred." It was just ten months later—on August 6, 1624—that *A Game at Chess* appeared.

It is first of all an ingenious play, a play in which the struggle between England and Spain, between Protestantism and Catholicism is described as a chess game. There is something a little like this perhaps in earlier Elizabethan and Jacobean plays that make incidental use of the symbolism of cards or bowling or chess. There is an example in *A Woman Killed with Kindness*, and there is of course the very striking example in Middleton's own *Women Beware Women*. But the symbolism is here by no means incidental; it runs through the whole play from the first scene to the last. The characters are grouped—when the two Houses meet—in the arrangement of the chess board; their costumes are white or black, according to the House they represent; their names are the names of the chess pieces, as the White Duke, the Black Knight, and the White Queen's Pawn. Their aim is to "take" members of the opposing House and ultimately to checkmate the opposing King. A vacant space when the Houses face one another indicates that a guilty pawn has stolen away; a character who is shown to wear a black shirt under his white outer garment is recognized as a hypocrite and a traitor. The whole play, in short, is a tour de force, which has even today the interest of novelty. It resembles modern plays that catch the attention of an audience by using an unorthodox technique.

The chief incident—or at least the incident that provides the climax—is a journey undertaken by the White Knight (Prince Charles) and the White Duke (the Duke of Buckingham). They visit the Black House, accept the entertainment that is lavished on them, and listen to a long exposé of Catholicism, delivered—oddly enough—by the chief spokesman of the Black King. The White Knight then announces checkmate "by discovery," and the characters of the Black House are stuffed into the bag. The whole episode is wildly improbable, but Middleton was obviously hard pressed to find a way of representing the Prince's journey to Madrid without touching directly on the Spanish marriage.

Several of the characters are probably intended as portraits of prominent Protestants and Catholics, but in only two cases —those of the Black Knight and the Fat Bishop—are the portraits very detailed. The Black Knight is clearly Count Gondomar. He is an unscrupulous politician with a sharp wit; he suffers from a fistula, he rides in a litter, and has a special chair. He reveals himself fully, if not in action, at least in soliloquy. He describes his plans for the universal monarchy, he discusses his ingratiating technique.

> And what I haue donne, I haue donne facetiouslie,
> Wth pleasant subteltie and bewitching Courtship
> Abusde all my Beleiuers wth delight
> They tooke a Comfort to bee coosned by mee,
> To manie a Soule, I haue let in mortall poyson
> Whose cheekes haue crackt wth laughter to receiue it.
>
> I.i.278–83

He has, he says, used the fleet of the White Kingdom, opened the jails and let out the Catholic locusts, muzzled the pulpit and press. But despite such transparent allusions to the activities of Gondomar, the Black Knight is essentially the Machiavellian villain of Jacobean tragedy. The Fat Bishop is de Dominis, Archbishop of Spalatro, who became a Protestant, found refuge in England, and subsequently returned to Rome. In the play he is represented as an arch-hypocrite, whose vanity and ambition are both boundless. He is not perhaps so distinguished a character as the Black Knight, but his appeal to a contemporary audience is easy to understand.[1]

About half the play is devoted to these Aristophanic por-

---

[1] The Fat Bishop was an afterthought on Middleton's part; he was not in the original draft of the play. See R. C. Bald, "An Early Version of Middleton's 'Game at Chesse,'" *Modern Language Review*, XXXVIII (July, 1943), 178.

traits; the other half tells a conventional story of injured innocence and miraculous escapes. The heroine is the White Queen's Pawn, who succumbs to Catholicism until she is almost raped by the Black Bishop's Pawn, her Jesuit confessor. Her cries for help are answered just in the nick of time. Subsequently she is persuaded that she can see her future husband in a magic glass—actually a mirror that reflects the Jesuit, now in disguise. She meets the impostor, accepts his advances, and enters a kind of marriage contract. But her virtue is again saved when he is tricked into spending the marriage night with another woman. Some of this is no doubt relevant to the theme of the play; Middleton is able to show that Jesuits are sometimes unscrupulous, that they abuse their authority, and that they adopt the strangest disguises. But the incidents are highly improbable, and the story is drawn out long after its satirical possibilities have been exhausted.

The dialogue is more uneven than is usual with Middleton, for he is obviously writing at top speed, obviously versifying any and every contemporary pamphlet on which he can lay his hands. An extreme example is the long discourse of the Black Knight in the final scene:

> Wee do not use to burie in our Bellyes
> 2 hundred thousand ducketts and then boast on't,
> Or exercize the ould Roman paynfull-Idlenes
> Wth care of fetching Fishes far from home,
> The Golden-headed Coracine out of AEgipt
> The Salpa from Eleusis, or the pelamis
> Wch some call Summer-Whiting from Calcedon,
> Salmons from Aquitayne, Helops from Rhodes,
> Cockles from Chios, franckt and fatted up
> Wth Far and Sapa flower and cockted wine,
> Wee cramb no birds, nor Epicurean-like
> Enclose some Creekes of the Sea, as Sergius Crata did
> Hee that inuented the first Stewes for Oysters

> And other Sea-Fish, who beside the pleasure
> Of his owne throate
> Got large Reuennewes by th' Inuentiõ,
> Whose Fat Example the Nobilitie followed.   V.iii.7–23

It is not like Middleton to parade his learning, and he would probably not have done so if he had had more time. But one should scarcely expect the most finished dialogue—or the most realistic action—in topical plays, even topical plays like *A Game at Chess* that brilliantly achieve their immediate purpose.

It is difficult to summarize the point of view of a man who wrote, beside poems, pamphlets, masques, and entertainments, at least twenty plays—some of them farces and some tragedies, some of them contemporary with the work of Marston and some with the work of Massinger and Ford. It is difficult, and T. S. Eliot has gone so far as to argue that it is really impossible.

Between the tragedies and the comedies of Shakespeare, and certainly between the tragedies and the comedies of Jonson, we can establish a relation; we can see, for Shakespeare or Jonson, that each had in the end a personal point of view which can be called neither comic nor tragic. But with Middleton we can establish no such relation. He remains merely a name, a voice, the author of certain plays, which are all of them great plays. He has no point of view, is neither sentimental nor cynical; he is neither resigned, nor disillusioned, nor romantic, he has no message. He is merely the name which associates six or seven great plays.[2]

Eliot is perhaps right when he distinguishes between Shakespeare and Jonson on the one hand and Middleton on the other, but he is not so clearly right when he refuses to say

[2] T. S. Eliot, *Selected Essays, 1917–1932* (New York: Harcourt, Brace, 1932), p. 141.

anything positive about Middleton or to see any relation between Middleton's comedies and tragedies. For surely there
is a relationship of a sort even between such different plays
as *A Mad World, My Masters* and *The Changeling*.

In both his earlier and his later drama Middleton is concerned, like Marston in *The Malcontent* and like Jonson in
Volpone, with vice rather than folly. He has a highly de-
veloped sense of sin, which rarely deserts him except perhaps
temporarily when he draws a Castiza to show how far short
of the ideal his other characters fall, or when, in some of the
tragicomedies, he digresses to study the weakness involved in
virtue itself. Sin is, in any case, his principal theme, appearing
in the farces, which contain some of the most despicable characters in English drama, in *The Revenger's Tragedy*, which
can well be called a nightmare of sin, and in the later tragedies, which deal characteristically with somewhat sordid pro-
tagonists.

Other Jacobean dramatists—not only Marston and Jonson, but Shakespeare, Webster, and Ford—deal from time
to time with the same theme. What is peculiar to Middleton
is his persistent concern with the irony that invests the sinner's
career. His thesis is that sin is blind. He wants to show that
the sinner inevitably gropes in a dark world until he stumbles
on the path that leads to inevitable disaster. Follywit who
pursues his grandfather's mistress, Lussurioso who turns for
help to his worst enemy, Beatrice who makes an accomplice
of the man she loathes—characters such as these epitomize
Middleton's ironic drama. As one follows them through the
plays in which they appear, one gets no doubt a sense of the
baseness of human nature, of which they are illustrations, but
one gets, too, a sense of the justice that prevails in the world
—a feeling for the mysterious moral force that closes their
eyes, misdirects their steps, and leads them to prepare their
own retribution. One discovers that sin is, in a very real sense,

a form of stupidity and that the sinner is a man who betrays himself.

Sin and retribution are not, of course, popular subjects, and Middleton never has been, perhaps never could be, exactly a popular writer. Compared with Dekker, he lacks humanity. There is very little sentiment in his work and perhaps less than adequate recognition of the warmer and kindlier human impulses. Compared to Webster, he lacks grandeur, partly at least because he refuses to compromise with sin. He never tolerates anything like the ambiguities reflected in the character of Flamineo, and if his Bianca occasionally resembles Vittoria Corombona, the two portraits are still measurably different, Webster's being much the more heroic. But if he is on the whole less moving than these writers, he is more satisfying intellectually. His vision seems clearer than theirs, his sense of reality more compelling. He offers a stern, a completely consistent and uncompromising view of human nature. As one reads him one is tempted to say: "This is true; so human beings behave; life and art have seldom been closer together." And one can rarely say the same thing of his most distinguished contemporaries, not even perhaps of Shakespeare.

Middleton is, as Eliot says, the author of six or seven great plays, and the number is about right. It should, I think, include *A Trick to Catch the Old One*, *A Mad World, My Masters*, and *The Revenger's Tragedy* from his earlier period, *A Chaste Maid in Cheapside*, *A Fair Quarrel*, *The Changeling*, *Women Beware Women*, and possibly *Hengist* from his later. But Middleton is more than this; he is the author of a large number of plays, some of them distinctly inferior no doubt, but most of them interesting as expressions of his state of mind at the time they were written, as reflections of a particular phase in the growth of his thought and the development of his art. He is, in short, a great writer in Eliot's sense—a man who has left a large body of work which forms a single pattern and expresses a single personality.

The standard set by Shakespeare is that of a continuous development from first to last, a development in which the choice both of theme and of dramatic and verse technique in each play seems to be determined increasingly by Shakespeare's state of feeling, by the particular stage of his emotional maturity at the time. What is "the whole man" is not simply his greatest or maturest achievement, but the whole pattern formed by the sequence of plays; so that we may say confidently that the full meaning of any one of his plays is not in itself alone, but in that play in the order in which it was written, in its relation to all of Shakespeare's other plays, earlier and later: we must know all of Shakespeare's work in order to know any of it.[3]

Middleton approaches this standard. He is not indeed another Shakespeare or another Jonson, but he stands above his other contemporaries. He is the third great dramatist of the Jacobean stage.

[3] T. S. Eliot, *Selected Essays, 1917–1932* (New York: Harcourt, Brace, 1932), p. 170.

Appendix

IN the following pages I have listed Middleton's works in more or less chronological order and referred to passages in Chambers and Bentley where information about dates, editions, sources, etc. can be found. When Chambers and Bentley are silent, I have given the information myself, and when they seem to me incomplete, I have added to what they say. My additions are most considerable where matters of authorship are concerned. I have avoided enumerating Middleton's "characteristics," partly because this has often been done before, and partly because I feel that to do so here would be to misrepresent the process of determining authorship, which is anything but deductive. One just does the best one can. One reads and forms, or tries to form, impressions; finally a play or a scene or a passage gets to "sound like" Middleton or Dekker or Rowley. Then one looks for somewhat more objective evidence that can be used to convince other readers. There is sometimes—as in the case of *The Revenger's Tragedy*—enough of this evidence, but more often there is not quite enough and what there is is not completely satisfactory.

NOTE ON TEXTS USED

Middleton, Thomas.
> *The Ghost of Lucrece.* Ed. Joseph Quincy Adams. New York and London, 1937.
>
> *A Game at Chesse.* Ed. R. C. Bald. Cambridge, 1929.
>
> *Hengist, King of Kent; or the Mayor of Queenborough.* Ed. R. C. Bald. New York and London, 1938.

The Honest Whore. Middleton, *Works*. Ed. Alexander Dyce. London, 1840.

The Revenger's Tragedy. Tourneur, *Works*. Ed. Allardyce Nicoll. London, 1929.

The Second Maiden's Tragedy 1611. Ed. W. W. Greg. Malone Society Reprints. Oxford, 1909.

Wit at Several Weapons. Beaumont and Fletcher, *Works*. Ed. Arnold Glover and A. R. Waller. Cambridge, 1905–12.

Other works: Middleton, *Works*. Ed. A. H. Bullen. London, 1885–86.

Dekker, Thomas.

Non-Dramatic Works. Ed. A. B. Grosart. London, 1884–86.

The Second Part of the Honest Whore. Middleton, *Works*. Ed. Dyce.

Other works: Dekker, *Dramatic Works*. London, 1873.

Rowley, William.

All's Lost by Lust and *A Shoemaker a Gentleman*. C. W. Stork, *William Rowley*. Philadelphia, 1910.

A Woman Never Vexed. Dodsley, *A Select Collection of Old English Plays*. Ed. W. C. Hazlitt. London, 1874–76.

Works Attributed to Middleton

Blurt, Master Constable and *The Spanish Gipsy*. Middleton, *Works*. Ed. Bullen.

The Meeting of Gallants at an Ordinary. Dekker, *Plague Pamphlets*. Ed. F. P. Wilson. Oxford, 1925.

The Nice Valor. Beaumont and Fletcher, *Works*. Ed. Glover and Waller.

The Puritan: The Shakespeare Apocrypha. Ed. C. F. Tucker Brooke. Oxford, 1908.

The Second Part of the Honest Whore. Middleton, *Works*. Ed. Dyce.

NOTE ON TITLES ABBREVIATED

Bentley: G. E. Bentley, *The Jacobean and Caroline Stage*. Oxford, 1941–56.

Bullen: Middleton, *Works*. Ed. A. H. Bullen. London, 1885–86.

Chambers: E. K. Chambers, *The Elizabethan Stage*. Oxford, 1923.

Dyce: Middleton, *Works*. Ed. Alexander Dyce. London, 1840.

Fleay: F. G. Fleay, *A Biographical Chronicle of the English Drama*. London, 1891.

Mermaid *Middleton: Thomas Middleton*. Mermaid Series. Ed. Havelock Ellis. London, 1887–90.

Schoenbaum: Samuel Schoenbaum, *Middleton's Tragedies, a Critical Study*. New York, 1955.

Stork: C. W. Stork, *William Rowley*. Philadelphia, 1910.

Wiggin: P. G. Wiggin, *An Inquiry into the Authorship of the Middleton-Rowley Plays*. Radcliffe College Monographs, No. 9. Boston, 1897.

MIDDLETON'S WORKS

1597
The Wisdom of Solomon Paraphrased

Authorship: In the introduction to the Mermaid *Thomas Middleton*, ed. Havelock Ellis (London, 1887–90), I, xxxii, Swinburne says that his author could never have written so bad a poem. Yet Middleton's full name occurs on the title-page; there can scarcely have been two Thomas Middletons who began to write at about the same time. The motto of the poem appears in the Stationers' Register for January 3, 1604, as part of the title of *The Ant and the Nightingale*, a work almost certainly Middleton's. See H. Dugdale Sykes, "Thomas Middleton's Early Non-Dramatic Work," *Notes and Queries*, CXLVIII (January–June, 1925), 435–38; *Ghost of Lucrece*, ed. Adams, pp. xiv–vi.

1599
Micro-Cynicon

Authorship: Swinburne is as definite about this poem as about *The Wisdom of Solomon Paraphrased.* "A lucid and melodious fluency of style is the mark of all [Middleton's] metrical writing: and this stupid piece of obscure and clumsy jargon could have been the work of no man endowed with more faculty of expression than informs or modulates the whine of an average pig" (Mermaid *Middleton*, I, xxxii). But the "Defiance to Envy" at the beginning is signed "T. M. Gent."—a signature also used in *The Ghost of Lucrece* and (without the Gent.) in *The Ant and the Nightingale* and *The Black Book.* See also H. Dugdale Sykes, "Thomas Middleton's Early Non-Dramatic Work," *Notes and Queries*, CXLVIII (January–June, 1925), 435–38.

1600
The Ghost of Lucrece

Critical edition: Ed. by Joseph Quincy Adams. New York and London, 1937.

Authorship: The initials "T. M." are on the title-page, and in the Latin invocation the author reveals his full name in the punning phrase *Thomas Medius & Grauis Tonus.* For further evidence, see the Adams edition, introduction.

1602(?)
The Family of Love

See E. K. Chambers, *The Elizabethan Stage* (Oxford, 1923), III, 440–41.

Date: The prologue suggests that this was an early play of the author's ("opinion hath not blaz'd his fame"), and the address to the reader says that it was not published for some time after it was written (when "the newness of it made it much more desired than at this time"). Thus an early date, say 1602–3, seems indicated, and the remarks in I.iii.101–13 about a play on Samson confirm this—such a play is mentioned by Henslowe (*Diary,* ed. Greg, I, 169) on July 29, 1602, and by the Duke of Stettin-Pomerania (C. W. Wallace, *The Children of the Chapel at Blackfriars 1597–1603* (Lincoln, 1908), p. 109, n. 1) on September 14, 1602. But there are also remarks in I.iii.109 and IV.iii.45–46 about a new company of porters, possibly one organized or reorganized in 1605; see Baldwin Maxwell, "A Note on the Date of Middleton's *The Family of Love,*" in *Elizabethan Studies and Other Essays in Honor of George F. Reynolds* (Boulder, 1945), pp. 195–200. This certainly complicates the matter and, along with other evidence, suggests that the play was revised several years after its original production.

Sources: By 1602 there was a large body of pamphlet literature dealing with contemporary manners, and it is quite possible that Middleton used it as material for *The Family of Love* and other plays. He may, for example, have taken suggestions for the incident of the mock court in Act V from Greene's *Notable Discovery of Cosenage* (1591) or from Rowlands' *Greene's Ghost Haunting Coney-Catchers* (1602) or from Chettle's *Kind-Harts Dreame* (1600)—the three possible sources are listed by Miss Fisher. But he may not have used any one of them—he may have been dramatizing a story he had heard. For this reason it seems better not to set down sources for the comedies unless one can be fairly sure of Middleton's indebtedness. For the whole matter, see R. C. Bald, "The Sources of Middleton's City Comedies," *Journal of English and Germanic Philology*, XXXIII (July, 1934), 373–87; M. G. Christian, "Middleton's Acquaintance with the *Merrie Conceited Jests of George Peele*," *PMLA*, L (September–December, 1935), 753–60; Christian, *Non-Dramatic Sources for the Rogues in Middleton's Plays* (Chicago, 1936); Margery Fisher, "Notes on the Sources of Some Incidents in Middleton's London Plays," *Review of English Studies*, XV (July, 1939), 283–93; and Signi Falk, "Plautus' *Persa* and Middleton's *A Trick to Catch the Old One*," *Modern Language Notes*, LXVI (January, 1951), 19–21.

Authorship: The play was first assigned to Middleton in the play lists of Archer (1656) and Kirkman (1661). It has since— or at least until quite recently—been universally accepted as his, though the dialogue is by no means all exactly in his manner. Some of the verse, for example—especially that in which Shakespeare and Marlowe are crudely imitated—seems more primitive than any in Middleton's other plays. Some of the prose, on the other hand, seems reasonably characteristic of him. Bald thinks that the play was revised, and though his evidence drawn from alternate names for the characters has been challenged, his theory certainly helps to explain the stylistic differences in the text. See W. J. Olive, "Imitation of Shakespeare in Middleton's *The Family of Love*," *Philological Quarterly*, XXIX (January, 1950), 75–78; R. C. Bald, "The Chronology of Middleton's Plays," *Modern Language Review*, XXXII (January, 1937), 36; and Maxwell, "A Note on the Date of Middleton's *The Family of Love*." Eberle explains the stylistic differences, or some of them, by supposing that Dekker helped with the play—that, in fact, Dekker's hand can be found in every scene except four short or fairly short ones (III.iv–vi and IV.i). He points out Dekker parallels, the closest, it seems to me, being these:

I.ii.41–42: let me be whipt to death with ladies' hair-laces.
Cf. *Old Fortunatus*, I, 136: let him bee shot to death with the terrible arrowes of faire Ladies eyes.

II.i.8–9: her soft pillow hath given her counsel to keep her bed.
Cf. *Gull's Hornbook*, II, 214–15: if you will but take sound councell of your pillow you shall neuer rise.

Generally, however, his evidence is not very convincing, since he relies too much on words and images that seem to him characteristic of Dekker or more characteristic of Dekker than of Middleton. I am not so much rejecting the theory of dual authorship as suggesting that, in the light of present knowledge, the theory of revision is at least as satisfactory. See Gerald J. Eberle, "Dekker's Part in *The Familie of Love*," in *Joseph Quincy Adams Memorial Studies* (Washington, 1948), pp. 723–38. I might add that Eberle's theory seems to me unnecessarily involved. *The Family of Love*, he says, "is a revision by Dekker and Middleton of an early play written by Middleton with considerable help from Dekker." See also Daniel B. Dodson, Thomas Middleton's City Comedies (unpublished Columbia dissertation, 1954), pp. 39–73, where a similar theory is advanced.

1603–4
The Phoenix

See Chambers, III, 439, and Baldwin Maxwell, "Middleton's *The Phoenix*," in *Joseph Quincy Adams Memorial Studies* (Washington, 1948), pp. 743–53.

1604
The Ant and the Nightingale; or Father Hubburd's Tales

S. R.: January 3, 1604.
Authorship: The address to the reader is signed "T. M."

1604
The Black Book

S. R.: March 22, 1604.
Authorship: Here too the address to the reader is signed with the initials "T. M."

1604
The Magnificent Entertainment

See Chambers, IV, 69–70.
Authorship: The piece is of course Dekker's and was published as his, but after the speech of Zeal, Dekker has the following note: "If there be any glory to be won by writing these lines, I do freely bestow it, as his due, on Tho. Middleton, in whose brain they were begotten, though they were delivered here: *quae nos non fecimus ipsi, vix ea nostra voco.*"

1604
The Honest Whore, with the Humors of the Patient Man and the Longing Wife

See Chambers, III, 294–95.
Authorship: At some time before March 14, 1604, Henslowe made the following entry in his *Diary* (I, 175): "Lent vnto the company to geue vnto Thomas deckers & midleton in earneste of ther playe Called the pasyent man & the onest hore the some of . . . vᴵᴵ." Clearly, then, Middleton was concerned in the play. Attempts to determine what his share was are to be found in the following works: Dyce, I, lvi, note; Bullen, I, xxvi; Mermaid *Middleton*, I, xxxv; Fleay, I, 131; A. W. Ward, *A History of English Dramatic Literature* (London, 1899), II, 462, note; M. L. Hunt, *Thomas Dekker, a Study* (New York, 1911), p. 100. The results can perhaps be arranged in the form of a table:

	Middleton	*Dekker*
Dyce:	"His share is comparatively small."	——
Bullen:	I.v; II.i; III.i.	The rest.
Swinburne:	Suggestions of M. in II.i.	——
Fleay:	I.ii, iv, v; II; III; IV.i–iii.	I.i, iii; IV.iv; V.
Ward:	Share not large; possibly "added some touches to the comic scenes."	——
Hunt:	Probably conceived the idea of the Candido plot; probably wrote I.v and III.i.	The rest.

Of the six authorities listed, five agree that the play is substantially Dekker's, and there is good reason for this. The play was published as his; it resembles his other work in plot, in characterization, and in style. The greater part of it can be Middleton's only if one is prepared to believe that Middleton was imitating Dekker, and there is no evidence that he did. Fleay gives none—in fact, Fleay gives no evidence at all for his fantastic scene-by-scene division of the play, which looks like pure guesswork.

What then did Middleton write? He may have written one or two of the Candido scenes; he may even have contributed to the scenes of Bellafront herself. But the evidence so far presented—as I think the following summary will show—is entirely inconclusive. *Candido scenes:* Hunt believes that Middleton was responsible for the "idea of the Candido plot" even though Dekker "held the pen." She points to the resemblance between Candido and two other Middleton characters—Quieto in an early play, *The Phoenix*, and Water-Camlet in a much later play, *Anything for a Quiet Life.* The resemblance between Candido and Quieto is certainly close; both illustrate humors—the same humor, in fact. But Middleton is not generally fond of humors, and it can scarcely be said that even Quieto is one of his more typical creations. Furthermore, Hunt's argument applies quite as well to the Candido of *The Second Part of the Honest Whore* as to the Candido of the first part, and it would be difficult indeed to maintain that Middleton was responsible for the second Candido. *II.i:* Bullen thinks that Middleton wrote the first of the Bellafront scenes because it resembles III.i in *Michaelmas Term.* But Bullen overlooks the fact that it also re-

sembles the first of the Imperia scenes in *Blurt, Master Constable*—
a play probably written by Dekker—and that Bellafront and Imperia are in some ways strikingly similar characters. "Trivia, strip
that villain; Simperina, pinch him, slit his wide nose. Fie, fie, fie,
I'll have you gelded for this lustiness." The speaker here is Imperia
and the villain referred to is Frisco, her servant. Yet Bellafront is
so fond of cursing Roger in precisely the same vein of whimsy that
the speech might easily be hers.

1604–6(?)
Your Five Gallants

See Chambers, III, 440.

Date: The play can scarcely have been written before 1604,
and if, as seems likely, it was originally a Paul's play, it cannot have
been written after the summer of 1606. The text may have been
revised, either before the original production or before a revival;
see R. C. Bald, "The Foul Papers of a Revision," *Library*, 4th
Series, XXVI (June, 1945), 37–50, and Baldwin Maxwell,
"Thomas Middleton's *Your Five Gallants*," *Philological Quarterly*, XXX (January, 1951), 30–39.

1604–6
Michaelmas Term

See Chambers, III, 440.

Date: The allusion in II.iii.226–29 has been much discussed,
but the authorities have not definitely decided whether it refers to
the execution of Francis Clarke at Winchester on November 29,
1603, or to the execution of Sir Everard Digby at the west end of
St. Paul's on January 30, 1606. See Dyce, I, 451, note; Fleay,
II, 91; and R. C. Bald, "The Chronology of Middleton's Plays,"
Modern Language Review, XXXII (January, 1937), 36. More
recently Maxwell has discovered another allusion in I.i.315–16—
the "sixpence British," pretty clearly the coinage with James's new
title of King of Great Britain, not in circulation until after November 11, 1604. See Baldwin Maxwell, "Middleton's *Michael-*

mas Term," *Philological Quarterly,* XXII (January, 1943), 29–35. Thus the play must have been written after November, 1604, and before the summer of 1606, when the Children of Paul's seem to have ceased acting.

Authorship: First assigned to Middleton by Archer and Kirkman. The central episode is similar to a passage in Dekker's *Lanthorn and Candlelight* (1608), and as an explanation of this Miss Teagarden has suggested very tentatively that "Dekker may have written the cheating scenes in the play." See Lucetta J. Teagarden, "The Dekker-Middleton Problem in *Michaelmas Term,"* in *Studies in English, Department of English, The University of Texas* (Austin, 1947), pp. 49–58.

1604–6
A Mad World, My Masters

See Chambers, III, 439–40.

1604–6
A Trick to Catch the Old One

See Chambers, III, 439.

1606–7
The Revenger's Tragedy

See Chambers, IV, 42.

Critical edition: Ed. by Allardyce Nicoll (*The Works of Cyril Tourneur*). London, 1929.

Source: The play seems to owe something to Florentine history —the poisoning of Luisa Strozzi and the murder of Alessandro de' Medici. See Samuel Schoenbaum, *Middleton's Tragedies, a Critical Study* (New York, 1955), pp. 9–11 and 228, where other authorities are listed.

Authorship: See my article, "The Authorship of the *Second Maiden's Tragedy* and *The Revenger's Tragedy,"* *Shakespeare Association Bulletin,* XX (April and July, 1945), 51–62, 121–33, and Schoenbaum, pp. 153–82, where much of my evidence is summarized; see also pp. 70–71 of the present text. I may perhaps be permitted at this point to say a word about E. H. C. Oliphant, the distinguished scholar who first presented the case for Middleton. He was right after all, and the scholars who for a generation now have ignored or sneered at his evidence, sometimes—when they have condescended to mention it—printing the word *evidence* itself between inverted commas, have not turned out to be our most reliable guides. But scholarship seldom divorces itself entirely from fashion, and what appeals to one generation—parallel passages, for example—is sometimes completely rejected by the next one. I should perhaps apologize for putting in more parallels here, but I am putting them in. Some are new and some have been rejected by Schoenbaum, presumably because he considers them "suspect."

I.ii.47:

A Rape! why tis the very core of lust.
Cf. *Michaelmas Term*, III.iv.266:
To beguile goodness is the core of sins.

I.ii.214:

I loue thy mischiefe well, but I hate thee.
Spurio is saying that he likes the sin but hates the sinner. Two characters in Middleton say the same thing—Bianca in *Women Beware Women*, II.ii.446–49:

and I'm like that great one,
Who, making politic use of a base villain,
He likes the treason well, but hates the traitor;
So I hate thee, slave!

and Proditor in *Phoenix*, II.ii.232:

I love the pearl thou sold'st, hate thee the seller.

II.i.8:

Why had not vertue a reuennewe?
Part of a soliloquy in which Castiza, introducing herself, complains about her poverty.
Cf. *No Wit*, I.ii.3: Has virtue no revenue? This is part of a

soliloquy in which Mistress Low-Water, introducing herself, complains about the same thing.

II.i.101:
> That forty Angells can make fourescore diuills.

Cf. *Family of Love*, I.ii.154: But angels make them admirable devils.

II.i.236:
> as vse-lesse as old men.

Cf. *Second Maiden's Tragedy*, l. 163:
> like an old man, thow canst doe nothing.

II.ii.280:
> The craftiest pleader gets most gold for breath.

Cf. *Ant and the Nightingale*, VIII, 106:
> Those pleaders . . .
> That wrestle with the arms of voice and air . . .
> Their innocent clients hist them on with gold.

II.ii.360:
> My haires are white, and yet my sinnes are Greene.

Cf. *Roaring Girl*, V.ii.124:
> Their sins are green even when their heads are grey.

III.v.2:
> O sweete, delectable, rare, happy, rauishing.

Cf. *More Dissemblers*, I.iv.100: O rich, ravishing, rare, and enticing!

III.v.77:
> Are Lord-ships sold to maintaine Lady-ships.

Oliphant compares *Phoenix*, II.ii.237–38:
> one that would sell
> His lordship if he lik'd her ladyship.

III.v.115–16:
> as faire a sine
> As some old gentlewoman in a Periwig.

Cf. *Family of Love*, II.ii.2–3: more lively and fresh than an old gentlewoman's glazed face in a new periwig.

III.vi.46–47:

> thinke of some Dame,
> Twill teach thee to dissemble.

V.i.119:

> Learne of our mother; lets dissemble to.

A common idea in Middleton; cf., for example, *Women Be-ware Women*, IV.ii.184–85:

> well, I had a mother,
> I can dissemble too.

IV.ii.110:

> Iue ene forgot what colour siluers off.

Cf. *Phoenix*, III.i.195–96: what colour's silver, I pray? you ne'er saw money in your life.

IV.ii.133–34:

> Ime couetuous
> To know the villayne.

Vindice wants to know the name of the man he is to murder. Cf. *Changeling*, II.ii.134, where De Flores wants to know the same thing:

> I thirst for him.

IV.iv.87–88:

> why, shee first begins with one,
> Who afterward to thousand prooues a whore.

Cf. *Changeling*, II.ii.60–64:

> for if a woman
> Fly from one point, from him she makes a husband,
> She spreads and mounts then like arithmetic;
> One, ten, a hundred, a thousand, ten thousand,
> Proves in time sutler to an army royal.

Also *Hengist*, IV.ii.274–79.

V.i.54:

> Thou art a mad beast.

II.ii.93:

> Thou'rt a mad apprehensiue knaue.

Lussurioso is responding to a joke. Characters in Middleton re-

spond to jokes in the same way; cf. *No Wit*, I.i.50 (Thou'rt
a mad slave), I.i.284 (You're not a mad knight), etc.

V.i.196–97:

>   A maske is treasons licence, that build vpon;
>   Tis murders best face when a vizard's on.

In *Women Beware Women* much the same thing is said about
the masque by Guardiano, IV.ii.163–66:

>   for mischiefs acted . . .
>   At the Duke's hasty nuptials, will be thought
>   Things merely accidental,

and by Bianca, V.i.62–63.

V.iii.90–91:

>   A piteous tragaedy, able to make
>   An old-mans eyes bloud-shot.

Cf. *Mad World*, III.ii.26–27: here's a sight able to make an
old man shrink!

1604–8(?)

The Roaring Girl; or Moll Cut-Purse

See Chambers, III, 296–97.

Date: At the end of the epilogue the authors promise that Moll
herself will appear on the Fortune stage, and it so happens that
she did appear—in 1604 or 1605. "Being at a play about three
quarters of a yeare since at *the* Fortune in mans apparel and in
her boots and *with* a sword at her syde, she told the company
then present *that* she thought many of them were of opinion that
she was a man, but if any of them would come to her lodging
they should finde she is a woman; and some other immodest and
lascivious speaches she also used at *that* time, and also sat upon
the stage in public viewe of all the people there present in mans
apparel and played upon her lute and sange a song": *Consistory
of London Correction Book* (1605–1606), under date 1605,
quoted in E. K. Chambers, "Elizabethan Stage Gleanings," *Review of English Studies*, I (January, 1925), 78. This certainly
tends to confirm the date of 1604–5, given in Fleay, I, 132. On
the other hand, there is even stronger evidence for 1607–8. V.i

shows close parallels with Dekker's *Belman of London* (S. R. March 14, 1608) and may well have been written at about the same time. Bald thinks that the "blazing star" of I.i.255 may be Halley's comet, which reached its perihelion toward the end of November, 1607. See R. C. Bald, "The Chronology of Middleton's Plays," *Modern Language Review*, XXXII (January, 1937), 37–38.

Authorship: In the First Part of *The Honest Whore* it is possible to pick out two or three scenes that Middleton might conceivably have written, but in *The Roaring Girl* it seems possible to do more—to identify definitely a number of scenes as Middleton's because they illustrate his style and express his point of view. The same thing can, I think, be done for Dekker, and I am therefore inclined to agree with Bullen, who says that in this play the shares of the two authors can be determined with some approach to exactness. See Dyce, I, lvi, note; Bullen, I, xxxvi–vii; Fleay, I, 132; A. W. Ward, *A History of English Dramatic Literature* (London, 1899), II, 519; Arthur Symons in the *Cambridge History of English Literature* (Cambridge, 1932), VI, 66; M. L. Hunt, *Thomas Dekker, a Study* (New York, 1911), pp. 111–12; H. Dugdale Sykes, *Sidelights on Elizabethan Drama* (London, 1924), p. 224; George R. Price, "The Shares of Middleton and Dekker in a Collaborated Play," *Papers of the Michigan Academy of Science, Arts, and Letters*, XXX (1944), 601–15.

	Middleton	Dekker	Middleton and Dekker
Dyce:	"By far the greater portion."	——	——
Bullen:	II.i; III ("mainly" M.); IV.i (possibly M.).	I; II.ii; V.	IV.ii ("M.'s for the most part, but the rhymed speeches at the end seem to belong to D.")
Fleay:	II.ii; IV.i; V.ii.	The rest.	——
Ward:	"Principal share."	——	——
Symons:	Underplot; little of Moll can be attributed to him.	Moll; Act V.	——
Hunt:	Same as Bullen.		
Sykes:	II.ii; IV.i.	IV.ii; V.i.	I; II.i; III; V.ii.
Price:	II.i–ii; III.i–ii; IV.i; V.ii.	IV.ii; V.i.	I; III.iii.

Bullen has a definite contribution to make, especially in the first
two scenes, but he is less trustworthy later. Fleay corrects Bullen's
errors but underestimates Middleton's share in the play. Sykes
corrects both his predecessors—in fact, his division is the most
satisfactory of those listed above. But he is perhaps a little too
cautious about three scenes, I, III.iii, and V.ii, all of which he
assigns to joint authorship.

The characters of the main plot look like Dekker's. The Roaring
Girl herself is another exercise in the sentimental manner of Bellafront, and the lovers, the melodramatic Sir Alexander Wengrave,
and the whimsical servants, Neatfoot and Trapdoor, can all be
paralleled in Dekker's other work. The characters in the subplot,
on the other hand, look like Middleton's, especially in II.i and
III.ii. They are drawn with his customary cynicism, and they
are, as Bullen says, just such characters as one finds in his other
plays. "Mistress Gallipot may be compared with Mistress Purge
in *The Family of Love* or with Falso's Daughter in *The Phoenix*;
and Mistress Openwork, the jealous scold, is a repetition of Mistress
Glister in *The Family of Love*." But in IV.ii there is, or seems to
be, a difference. The unfaithful wife and the jealous scold turn
out to be quite amiable after all—perhaps an indication that Dekker
took over the subplot at this point.

The evidence of the characterization suggests a rough division
of the play—a main plot written by Dekker and a subplot written
in collaboration. But other sorts of evidence show that the case
is not so simple as this. Middleton was certainly concerned in
the main plot, and Dekker's contribution to the subplot was not
confined to IV.ii. But the evidence should perhaps be considered
scene by scene.

I. Dekker: There is nothing here that sounds like Middleton and
much that seems certainly Dekker—the description of the theatre,
the whimsical speeches of Neatfoot, the tender speeches of the
lovers, the persiflage about chairs in ll. 167–80 (cf. *Satiromastix*,
I, 203–4), and Sir Alexander's long narrative. Dekker is fond
of chorus speeches—that is, speeches headed *All, Both,* etc.—and
there are several of them in this scene. Dekker parallels:

72–74:

> my thoughts must run
> As a horse runs that's blind round in a mill,
> Out every step, yet keeping one path still.

Cf. *Northward Ho*, III,17:

> and I that like a horse
> Ran blind-fold in a Mill (all in one circle).

But see *Game at Chess*, I.i.12 (Yet misse the path shee can run blindefold in).

80–82:

> 'tis in heaven's book
> Set down, that I must have thee; an oath we took
> To keep our vows.

Cf. *Satiromastix*, I, 210:

> I dare and will by that ioynt holy oath,
> Which she and I swore to the booke of heauen.

Also *Satiromastix*, I, 254 (the booke of heauen) and *Wonderful Year*, I, 88 (the booke of heauen).

197–98:

> Fortune, who slaves men, was my slave; her wheel
> Hath spun me golden threads.

Cf. *Whore of Babylon*, II, 219:

> fine and golden threds
> Are drawne and spun (for them) by the good fates.

Also *If This Be Not a Good Play*, III, 348 (Here we begin/ Our reigne anew, which golden threds shall spin) and *Lust's Dominion* (Dodsley, *A Select Collection of Old English Plays*, ed. W. C. Hazlitt, London, 1874–76), XIV, 167 (The destinies have spun a silken thread/ About my life).

356–58:

> —Play thou the subtle spider; weave fine nets
> To ensnare her very life.
>   —Her life?
>   —Yes; suck
> Her heart-blood, if thou canst.

Cf. *Whore of Babylon*, II, 195:
> O t'is a cunning Spider,
> And in her nets so wraps the Fairie Queene,
> That shee suckes euen her breast.

II.i. Middleton and Dekker: The greater part of the dialogue seems definitely Middleton's, but after Moll's entrance there appear to be touches of Dekker. Dekker parallels:

235–37: I send you for hollands, and you're i' th' low countries, with a mischief.
Cf. *Northward Ho*, III, 65: maister cittiner sleepes as quietly, as if he lay in his owne low-country of *Holland*, his own linnen I meane sir.

245–47: — . . . I'll show you mine arms when you please, sir. —I had rather see your legs, and begin that way.
Cf. *Blurt*, I.i.90–91: — . . . talk of any subject but this jangling law at arms. —The law of legs then. Also *1 Honest Whore*, III, 120: give me thy golls,/ We'll talk of legs hereafter.

284–88: —Prithee, sweet, plump Moll, when shall thou and I go out a' town together?—Whither? to Tyburn, prithee? —Mass, that's out a' town indeed: thou hangest so many jests upon thy friends still! In F. E. Pierce, *The Collaboration of Webster and Dekker* (New York, 1909), p. 76, this is compared to *Northward Ho*, III, 11: —If thou't haue a lodging West-ward Doll, Ile fitte thee. —At Tyburne will you not? a lodging of your prouiding?

II.ii. Middleton and Dekker(?): This scene, Bullen says, "has Dekker's naturalness of sentiment and fluency of metre, a not unpleasing mixture of blank verse and rhyme." I think Bullen is wrong—it seems to me that the style in the greater part of the scene is identifiable as Middleton's—but the clock passage in lines 111–21 might well be Dekker's. It is fairly close to *2 Honest Whore*, III, 173. On the other hand, it is equally close to *Women Beware Women*, IV.i.1–18 (written in imitation of Dekker?). See p. 204 for clock passages in *Your Fire Gallants* and *The Black Book*; see also *Mad World*, IV.i.20–24.

III.i. Middleton and Dekker(?): The fishing image in Moll's long speech may well be Dekker's; he is fond of the idea of hooks or nets made of precious metal, especially fond of the phrase "golden hooks." But much of the dialogue seems to be Middleton's.

III.ii. Middleton and Dekker: The prose at the beginning looks like Middleton's, and the incident of the pre-contract is, as Bullen says, duplicated in Middleton's play, *A Trick to Catch the Old One.* But there is also evidence for Dekker—the oaths *God's-so* and *uds light,* the ejaculation *tush,* and the moon passage.

125–26:
> Since last I saw him, twelve months three times told
> The moon hath drawn through her light silver bow.

Dyce compares *Whore of Babylon,* II, 195:
> Fiue Summers haue scarce drawn their glimmering nights
> Through the Moons siluer bowe.

Cf. also 2 *Honest Whore,* III, 223 (The moon hath through her bow scarce drawn to th' head,/ Like to twelve silver arrows, all the months) and *Whore of Babylon,* II, 246 (The Moone that from your beames did borrow light,/ Hath from her siluer bow shot pitchy clowds).

III.iii. Dekker: The tone and much of the imagery seem to be Dekker's and there are chorus speeches. As far as I can see, the only evidence for Middleton is the pun on *mace* in l. 178, which occurs in *A Mad World,* III.ii.75–76, and *Anything for a Quiet Life,* III.ii.20–21, but also in *Westward Ho,* II, 359. Dekker parallels:

73–75:
> Right: but I have in my brain
> A windmill going that shall grind to dust
> The follies of my son.

In *The Merry Devil of Edmonton 1608,* ed. W. A. Abrams (Durham, 1942), pp. 77–78, this is compared to *Virgin Martyr,* IV, 28 (Thy head is full of Wind-mils), *Witch of Edmonton,* IV, 410 (Some Wind-mill in my brains), etc.

172–73: What toads are these to spit.poison on a man to his face! Cf. *Lanthorn and Candlelight*, III, 213: & hauing sucked what knowledge he can from them, to turne it al into poison, & to spit it in the verie faces of the professors.

197–200: Some poor, wind-shaken gallant will anon fall into sore labour, and these men-midwives must bring him to bed i' the Counter: there all those that are great with child with debts lie in.

Dyce compares *Whore of Babylon*, II, 213: Doe not you know (mistresse) what Serieants are? . . . why they are certaine men-midwiues, that neuer bring people to bed, but when they are sore in labour, that no body else can deliuer them.

IV.i. Middleton: Perhaps the most that can be said about this scene is that it occasionally sounds like Middleton but never like Dekker. Middleton parallel:

151:
    No poison, sir, but serves us for some use.
    Cf. *Women Beware Women*, I.ii.182–83:
        providence, that has made every poison
    Good for some use.
    Also *Changeling*, II.ii.43–44 (the ugliest creature/ Creation fram'd for some use).

IV.ii. Dekker: The behavior of the characters (particularly Mistress Gallipot and Mistress Openwork), the style, and the versification all point to Dekker. There are chorus speeches. Dekker parallels:

206–10:
    Thou spider that hast woven thy cunning web
    In mine own house t' ensnare me! hast not thou
    Suck'd nourishment even underneath this roof,
    And turn'd it all to poison, spitting it
    On thy friend's face.
    See notes on I.i.356–58 and III.iii.172–73.

281–82: Nay, gentlemen, seeing your women are so hot, I must lose my hair in their company, I see. [*Takes off his false hair.*] Pierce compares 2 *Honest Whore*, III, 167; Nay, if your service be so hot a man cannot keep his hair on, I'll serve you no longer. See also *Westward Ho*, II, 362: Looke you, your Schoole-maisier has bin in *France*, and lost his hayre.

319–20:
    —Play out your game at Irish, sir: who wins?
    —The trial is when she comes to bearing.
Dyce compares *Northward Ho*, III, 54: did not I tell you old man, that sheed win my game when she came to bearing?

V.i. Dekker: This scene seems so obviously Dekker's that detailed evidence is unnecessary. There are many parallels with *The Belman of London*.

V.ii. Middleton: Bullen gives this scene entirely to Dekker, Sykes to Dekker and Middleton. But it is hard to see what part of it Dekker might have written, except perhaps the line singled out by Abrams: "I find it in the music of my heart." The style seems to me Middleton's.

1609
Sir Robert Sherley's Entertainment in Cracovia

S. R.: May 30, 1609, as "the travells of Sir Robert Sherley."
Authorship: The dedication to Sir Robert's brother, Sir Thomas Sherley, is signed—in certain copies at least—"Thomas Middleton."

1611
The Second Maiden's Tragedy

See Chambers, IV, 45.
Source: The subplot comes from the "Story of the One Who Was Too Curious for His Own Good" in *Don Quixote*. See Schoenbaum, pp. 38–49.

Authorship: See my article, "The Authorship of the *Second Maiden's Tragedy* and *The Revenger's Tragedy*," *Shakespeare Association Bulletin*, XX (April and July, 1945), 51–62, 121–33, and Schoenbaum, pp. 183–202.

1611<
A Chaste Maid in Cheapside

See Chambers, III, 441.

Date: On the title-page of the first edition the play is described as having been acted by the Lady Elizabeth's Men, a company apparently formed in 1611. The scene of the promoters and the "religious wholesome laws" mentioned in Touchwood's speech II.i.109–13 suggest that Middleton was writing while a special effort was being made to enforce the observance of Lent. In "The Chronology of Middleton's Plays," *Modern Language Review*, XXXII (January, 1937), 39–40, R. C. Bald shows that special enforcement measures were taken by the Privy Council and the Lord Mayor early in 1613.

Source: Middleton possibly got suggestions for Allwit (and for Sophonirus in *The Second Maiden's Tragedy*) from an epigram in Campion's *Observations in the Art of English Poesy* (1602). See E. L. Buckingham, "Campion's *Art of English Poesie* and Middleton's *Chaste Maid in Cheapside*," *PMLA*, XLIII (September, 1928), 784–92.

(?)
Wit at Several Weapons

See Chambers, III, 232.

Authorship: See R. Boyle, "Beaumont, Fletcher and Massinger," *Englische Studien*, VIII (1885), 51–52; Fleay, I, 218; Macaulay in the *Cambridge History of English Literature* (Cambridge, 1932), VI, 138; A. H. Thorndike, *The Influence of Beaumont and Fletcher on Shakspere* (Worcester, 1901), pp. 87–88; C. M. Gayley, *Beaumont, the Dramatist* (New York, 1914), p. 378; M. Chelli, *Étude sur la collaboration de Massinger*

avec Fletcher et son groupe (Paris, 1926), p. 306; E. H. C.
Oliphant, *The Plays of Beaumont and Fletcher* (New Haven,
1927), pp. 451–57; Dewar M. Robb, "The Canon of William
Rowley's Plays," *Modern Language Review*, XLV (April, 1950),
137–38; William W. Appleton, *Beaumont and Fletcher, a Critical
Study* (London, 1956), p. 47.

Boyle: Fletcher and a collaborator.
Fleay: Fletcher and Rowley.
Macaulay: Middleton and Rowley.
Thorndike: Pompey part probably Beaumont's.
Gayley: No Beaumont in the play.
Chelli: Beaumont and Fletcher.
Wells: Middleton: I.i; III; IV. Rowley: the rest.
Oliphant: Beaumont, Fletcher, Middleton, and possibly Rowley.
Robb: Mostly Middleton but Rowley in II.ii–iii and V.i–ii, possibly
               also in II.iv.
Appleton: "Almost certainly belongs largely to Middleton."

The external evidence for Beaumont and Fletcher is fairly
strong. The play was published in the first folio of their work
and later entered as theirs in the S. R. It is ascribed to them in
Archer's play list. In the folio text the epilogue, written "at the
reviving of this Play," mentions Fletcher as one of the authors.
Nevertheless, it is rather difficult to find either Beaumont or
Fletcher in the text that has come down to us, and rather easy
to find Middleton. I am inclined to agree with the scholars listed
above who credit him with a substantial share in the play.

The best evidence for Middleton is the fact that the story of
Wittypate and Sir Perfidious resembles in a general way the story
of Witgood and Lucre in *A Trick to Catch the Old One* and the
story of Follywit and Sir Bounteous in *A Mad World, My Masters.*
In all three plays a young man engages in an ironic contest with
a father, grandfather, or uncle. In *Wit at Several Weapons* the
irony is particularly pointed in the first part of IV.i, a scene that
is in many ways reminiscent of Middleton's best work. The story
of Cunningham, the Niece, and the Fool, however, is much
less characteristic; any one of a number of authors might conceivably have written it.

A style that reads very much like Middleton's appears in I.i (pp. 66–74 in Glover and Waller), II.i (pp. 82–83), III, and IV. The percentage of feminine endings is high in these scenes, and there are parallels with Middleton's work. In II.i, p. 82, for example, the author introduces Lady Ruinous Gentry much as Middleton introduces Mistress Low-Water in I.ii of *No Wit, No Help Like a Woman's*. Both characters deliver a long speech on the difficulties that beset distressed gentlewomen. A few other parallels follow:

II.i, p. 82:
   Fed with a wound upon me, stampt at midnight.
   Cf. *Hengist*, V.ii.111:
   What, has thy wild rage stampt a wound vpon me.
   Also *Widow*, V.i.128 (a sin stampt last midnight) and *Women Beware Women*, IV. ii. 37–38 (a wound lately/ Of a base stamp upon me).

III.i, p. 99:
   There is no boldness like the impudence
   That's lockt in a fools bloud.
   Cf. *Second Maiden's Tragedy*, ll. 250–51:
   you shall not want content, if it be lockt
   in any blood of myne.
   Also *Old Law*, IV.ii.206–7 (For he that gives us life first, as a father,/ Locks all his natural sufferings in our blood).

III.i, p. 100:
   A pox upon that wrangling, say I still. . . .
   It fights i' th' tongue, but sure to agree i' th' haunches.
   Cf. *Changeling*, II.i.86:
   Wrangling has prov'd the mistress of good pastime.
   Another style—one that is sometimes reminiscent of Rowley's —appears in I.ii (pp. 74–81), II.ii–iv (pp. 83–97), and V. There are far fewer feminine endings here but at least an equal number of Rowley parallels.

II.ii, p. 89:
   I took thee down a little way to
   Enforce a Vomit from my offended stomach.

Cf. *Fair Quarrel*, V.i.11–12:
You can give yourself a vomit to return 'em
If they offend your stomach.

II.ii, p. 92:
He cannot freeze at such a flaming beauty.
Cf. *Changeling*, III.iii.181–82:
How can he freeze
Lives near so sweet a warmth?

II.ii, p. 92:
Oh I should climb my Stars, and sit above.
Cf. *All's Lost by Lust*, V.v.191:
Our soules climbe stars.

II.ii, p. 92:
To see him burn to ashes in his love.
Cf. *Fair Quarrel*, I.i.356–57:
O this fire will flame me
Into present ashes!

I am perhaps suggesting that the play is an example of the collaboration of Middleton and Rowley, but the evidence scarcely warrants so definite a conclusion. All one can be reasonably sure of is that Middleton himself had something to do with it.

1613
Entertainment at the Opening of the New River

See Chambers, III, 443.

1613
The Triumphs of Truth

See Chambers, III, 443.
Sources: For Middleton's indebtedness to Jonson and Dekker, see Celeste Turner, *Anthony Mundy, an Elizabethan Man of Letters,* University of California Publications in English (Berkeley, 1928), II, No. 1, 160.

1610<
No Wit, No Help Like a Woman's

See Chambers, III, 441.

Date: The play shows the influence of Beaumont and Fletcher, and can scarcely have been written before the second decade of the century.

Source: The underplot comes from Giambattista della Porta's *La Sorella*. See *Critical Essays of the Seventeenth Century,* ed. J. E. Spingarn (Oxford, 1908–9), II, 335, and D. J. Gordon, "Middleton's *No Wit, No Help Like a Woman's* and della Porta's *La Sorella,*" *Review of English Studies,* XVII (October, 1941), 400–14.

Authorship: C. W. Stork, *William Rowley* (Philadelphia, 1910), pp. 47–48, finds traces of Rowley, particularly in III and IV.ii, where Pickadill appears.

c. 1610–16(?)
The Witch

See Bentley, IV, 903–5.

c. 1616
The Widow

See Chambers, III, 442, and Bentley, IV, 900–3.

Authorship: See *A Select Collection of Old Plays,* new ed., ed. Reed, Gilchrist, and [J. P. Collier] (London, 1825–27), XII, 215; Bullen, I, lxxxvi–vii; Fleay, II, 106; *Cambridge History of English Literature* (Cambridge, 1932), VI, 65 (Symons), 140 (Macaulay); E. H. C. Oliphant, *The Plays of Beaumont and Fletcher* (New Haven, 1927), pp. 492–98; W. J. Lawrence, *Speeding Up Shakespeare* (London, 1937), pp. 106–13; Jonson, *Works,* ed. C. H. Herford, Percy and Evelyn Simpson (Oxford, 1925–52), X, 338–40.

Collier:	Opening of the play is in Middleton's manner. Act IV: Jonson.
Bullen:	Possibly revised by Fletcher, though no evidence for either Fletcher or Jonson.
Fleay:	Middleton, possibly revised by Fletcher and Jonson.
Symons:	Nothing of Jonson; Fletcher might have revised the play and written one or two of the songs.
Macaulay:	Probably all Middleton.
Oliphant:	"Practically wholly Middleton's," though perhaps some Fletcher in IV.i and V.i.
Lawrence:	Middleton, Jonson, and Fletcher.
Herford and Simpson:	"No sign of Jonson's hand."
Bentley:	"If Fletcher or Jonson had any part . . . it must have been slight."

The names of Jonson, Fletcher, and Middleton appear on the title-page of the first edition, but in one copy the first two names have been struck out in an old hand and the word *alone* has been written after the name of Middleton; see Dyce, III, 339. Archer attributes the play to Middleton alone, Kirkman to Middleton and Rowley.

Despite the fact that the play appears in neither of the Beaumont and Fletcher folios, there is some reason for thinking that Fletcher was concerned in it. The plot is in his manner—much more in his manner, in fact, than in Middleton's. But there is, as far as I can see, no stylistic evidence for Fletcher. Whether he outlined the play and left Middleton to write it, or whether Middleton deliberately imitated him will perhaps never be known. I am unable to find any internal evidence for Jonson.

1616
Civitatis Amor

See Chambers, III, 443–44.

Authorship: Middleton's signature occurs at the end of "The Entertainment at Whitehall." Presumably he did not write the following part called "Prince Charles His Creation."

1617
The Triumphs of Honor and Industry

See Bentley, IV, 897.

>1623
More Dissemblers Besides Women

See Bentley, IV, 888–89.

1615(?)–17
A Fair Quarrel

See Bentley, IV, 867–70.

Authorship: Bullen, I, xliv; Mermaid *Middleton*, I, xxi–ii; Fleay, II, 98; P. G. Wiggin, *An Inquiry into the Authorship of the Middleton-Rowley Plays*, Radcliffe College Monographs, No. 9 (Boston, 1897), pp. 29–39; Stork, pp. 39–41; E. H. C. Oliphant, *Shakespeare and His Fellow Dramatists* (New York, 1929), II, 807–49; W. D. Dunkel, "Did Not Rowley Merely Revise Middleton?" *PMLA*, XLVIII (September, 1933), 799–805; Dewar M. Robb, "The Canon of William Rowley's Plays," *Modern Language Review*, XLV (April, 1950), 130, 137.

	Middleton	*Rowley*
Bullen:	II.i and III.i; "scenes where Captain Ager and the Colonel are concerned."	End of I; Jane-Fitzallen scenes; boisterous comic scenes.
Swinburne:	—	Underplot.
Fleay:	I (part); II.i, iii; III.ii; IV.ii, iii; V (part).	I (part); II.ii; III.ii; IV.i, iv; V (part).
Wiggin:	Main plot, except I.	Underplot and I.
Stork:	Same as Wiggin.	
Oliphant:	Same as Wiggin, except that the first five or six speeches in I tentatively given to Middleton.	
Dunkel:	Middleton wrote the play and Rowley revised it.	
Robb:	Rowley planned the play and did most of the original writing; Middleton wrote the chief scenes and revised Rowley's work. In his detailed division Robb follows Wiggin, except that he gives Middleton the first two pages at least of I and the last	

two of V. He is not sure about IV.ii but inclined to think it unlike Rowley.

Except for Fleay and Dunkel, the authorities substantially agree, and there is reason to think that Fleay differs from the others only where his division is marred by misprints. The main plot is clearly Middleton's; it is marked as his by the irony, by the richness of the characterization, and by the mastery of the style. The subplot and the comic scenes are just as clearly Rowley's. The only real problem is I, where the characters of both plots appear. At the beginning the scene looks like Middleton's—at least the style and the versification seem to be his. But after the first 30 lines there are unmistakable indications of Rowley: the motivation is crude, the verse is rough, feminine endings are comparatively rare.

Wiggin notices Rowley parallels in I.i.122–23 (cf. the dedication signed by Rowley) and V.i.5–6 (cf. *All's Lost by Lust*, IV.i.72–73). There are other Rowley parallels in II.ii.65–66 (cf. *Shoemaker a Gentleman*, I.iii.48), V.i.10–12 (cf. *Shoemaker*, II.i.45–46), and V.i.308–9 (cf. *Shoemaker*, III.ii.109–10).

1616(?)<
Hengist, King of Kent; or the Mayor of Quinborough

See Bentley, IV, 883–87.

c. 1618(?)
The Old Law; or a New Way to Please You

See Bentley, IV, 889–91.

Authorship: See Bullen, I, xv–xvii; Mermaid *Middleton*, I, xxii; Fleay, II, 100–1; E. C. Morris, "On the Date and Composition of *The Old Law*," *PMLA*, XVII (1902), 1–70; Stork, p. 49; A. H. Cruickshank, *Philip Massinger* (Oxford, 1920), pp. 141–42; Dewar M. Robb, "The Canon of William Rowley's Plays," *Modern Language Review*, XLV (April, 1950), 136–37; George R. Price, "The Authorship and the Manuscript of *The Old Law*," *Huntington Library Quarterly*, XVI (February, 1953), 117–39.

	Middleton	Rowley	Massinger
Bullen:	"All the serious parts"; the talk of the lawyers (I), the court gallants and Eugenia (II. ii; III.ii); and V (part).	Share "considerable." III.i; V (Gnotho).	Probably "did no more than" revise the play; "I doubt whether he added a single scene."
Swinburne:	"Finer passages."	"Farcical interludes."	—
Fleay:	—	Creon-Antigona parts: I; II.i; V.	Hard to recognize.
Morris:	Wrote original play.	Revised it.	Revised the revision.
Stork:	Treats the theme "wittily."	Gnotho; also I (Creon-Antigona); II.i; III.ii (Simonides); V (Creon-Antigona).	Treats the theme "seriously."
Cruickshank:	—	—	Possibly revised the play.
Robb:	Share in all scenes except IV.i.	IV.i; share in all other scenes except III.ii and IV.ii.	Share in all scenes except II.ii; III.i; and IV.i.
Price:	II.ii; III.i. Middleton revised by Massinger: I; III. ii; and IV.ii.	IV.i. Rowley revised by Massinger: II.i and V.	Revised I; II.i; III. ii; IV.ii; and V.

Bullen succeeds in showing that the Gnotho scenes were written by Rowley; otherwise not much progress is recorded in the first part of the foregoing table. Fleay gives no evidence for his assignments, and Morris—who divides up the play almost line by line—gives no evidence that can be taken seriously. The weakness of his method is pretty clearly revealed in his introduction to *The Spanish Gipsy*, where he divides between Middleton and Rowley (again line for line) a play the greater part of which was very probably written by Ford. Stork begins with a general statement (which I may have misinterpreted in my table of authorship): The theme of *The Old Law* is "treated seriously, wittily and farcically by three sets of characters. Roughly these three treatments may represent respectively Massinger, Middleton and Rowley." Later he seems to give III.ii to Rowley because the character of Simonides "has some of Rowley's daring, and perpetuates a pun too odious for either of the other collaborators." But later still he confesses his doubts. The characters are hopelessly mixed up, he says. "I would not venture to assign anything positively to Rowley except the Gnotho scenes, the most successful part of the play." Cruickshank is reminded of Massinger in isolated speeches —among them a speech in which the marks of Middleton's style seem to me pretty clear. Morris, Robb, and Price are the only authorities listed above who have no difficulty in recognizing Massinger and who are indeed prepared to assign him a substantial share in the play. Robb offers no evidence, for Massinger at least, and Price offers very little.

The play is undoubtedly the most difficult one of the Middleton-Rowley group. It may have been revised, and in any case there is a third author who has to be considered. The text is bad, and it is possible that what now looks like Rowley may sometimes be corrupt Middleton or even corrupt Massinger. Nevertheless, I feel that the principal contributions of Rowley and Middleton can still be identified. I am not so sure about Massinger, who may not have been concerned in the play at all.

The irony which invests the story of Hippolita strongly suggests Middleton, and the character of Eugenia resembles several characters in Middleton's other plays. I suspect, therefore, that he was at least principally responsible for II.ii, III.ii, and IV.ii. The scenes of Gnotho are probably Rowley's, and the scenes of Simonides and Creon—in which villainy and injured innocence clash—are very probably his too. I should therefore give him the greater part of II.i, III.i, IV.i, and V (after Gnotho's entrance). I am not quite sure about the first act, though Rowley was certainly concerned in it and may have written it all. The trial scene, V (before Gnotho's entrance), does not seem to be Middleton's and may not be Rowley's.

Verse tests are worth something, though not perhaps very much ("worse than useless," Robb says) in a play so badly printed. By my count the percentage of feminine endings is high in II.ii, III.ii, and IV.ii—the scenes that on other grounds I have assigned to Middleton—and low in I and V. Hard words are scattered through the play and usually appear in scenes that on other grounds would be assigned to Rowley. It is certainly difficult to imagine Middleton using *predecessive* (I.i.69), *vegetives* (I.i.325), *reluctations* (I.i.331), or *obits* (I.i.466).

I. Rowley and Middleton (?): There are a few suggestions of Middleton here but (despite Price) very little of the scene can be his. Rowley parallel:

72–73:
> O lad, here's a spring for young plants to flourish!
> The old trees must down kept the sun from us.

Cf. *Changeling*, I.ii.22–25:—Old trees and young plants often grow together,/ Well enough agreeing. —Ay, sir, but the old trees raise themselves higher and broader than the young plants.

II.i. Middleton and Rowley: The long speech of Cleanthes (lines 169–97) is probably Middleton's; such lines as

> 'tis joy clad like a joy,
> Which is more honest than a cunning grief,

are particularly characteristic. But there are other speeches that can only have been written by Rowley. Rowley parallel:

161–63:
> I ha' known a widow laugh closely, my lord,
> Under her handkercher, when t'other part
> Of her old face has wept like rain in sunshine.

Cf. *All's Lost*, V.v.96–97:
> Why? hast never seene the sun-shine of a rainy day?
> Who does beleeve a widows teares to be her hearts sorrow?

II.ii. Middleton: The style here seems to be Middleton's throughout.

III.i. Rowley (?): I feel something less than complete conviction about this scene, which may, as Price says, be Middleton's.

III.ii. Middleton: Middleton parallels:

208–17:
> look, look, his face
> Is set for stormy weather; do but mark

How the clouds gather in't, 'twill pour down straight. . . .
I told you there would be a shower anon.
Cf. *Women Beware Women*, III.ii.30–31:
The storm is now in's heart, and would get nearer,
And fall here, if it durst; it pours down yonder.
Also *Changeling*, II.i.51–58:
And I'll endure all storms before I part with't. . . .
Now't begins again;
I'll stand this storm of hail, though the stones pelt me . . .
The shower falls amain now.

254–55:
As from a priest to steal a holy vestment,
Ay, and convert it to a simple [sinful: Dyce] covering.
Cf. *More Dissemblers*, V.ii.227–28:
Steal'st thou a holy vestment from religion
To clothe forbidden lust with?

267–68:
thou'rt a disease
That stick'st to th'heart.
Cf. *More Dissemblers*, III.i.128–30:
no man's hate
Can stick more close unto a loath'd disease
Than mine to him.

IV.i. Rowley. IV.ii. Middleton: Middleton parallels:

35–36:
I've a joy weeps to see you, 'tis so full,
So fairly fruitful.
Bullen compares *Changeling*, III.iv.25–26:
our sweet'st delights
Are evermore born weeping.

52–53:
never son
Was in the way more of celestial rising.
Spoken as a kneeling character rises.

Cf. *Second Maiden's Tragedy*, ll. 813–14, where a kneeling character also rises:

> and maye it proue
> the first asscent of your ymortall risinge.

V. Rowley: In the first part of the scene—the episode of the trial—there are a few lines that might have been written by Middleton, 250–51, for example. But there is no good evidence for his hand and not much for Rowley's. In the last part, however—the episode of Gnotho—the marks of Rowley are unmistakable. Rowley parallels:

36:

> You shall no longer bosom January.

Robb compares *Woman Never Vexed*, XII, 163: January and May! I for a younger tarry.

87:

> My stomach strives [strikes: Gifford] to dinner.

Robb compares *Shoemaker*, I.ii.183: The chimes of my belly has gone.

1618
The Peacemaker; or Great Britain's Blessing

Authorship: On July 19, 1618, the *Calendar of State Papers, Domestic* records: "Licence to Wm. Alley, at nomination of Thomas Middleton, of the sole printing and publishing of a book by Middleton called *The Peace-maker, or Great Britain's Blessing.*" See Bullen, I, xliv–v.

1619
The Inner-Temple Masque; or Masque of Heroes

See Bentley, IV, 881–82.

1619
On the Death of Richard Burbage

First printed in J. P. Collier, *New Facts Regarding the Life of Shakespeare* (London, 1835), p. 26.

1619
The Triumphs of Love and Antiquity

See Bentley, IV, 899.

1619–20

The World Tossed at Tennis

See Bentley, IV, 907–11.

Authorship: See Fleay, II, 100; Wiggin, pp. 39–40; Stork, p. 41; Dewar M. Robb, "The Canon of William Rowley's Plays," *Modern Language Review*, XLV (April, 1950), 138–39.

	Rowley	*Middleton*
Fleay:	First part.	Last part.
Wiggin:	Up to the entrance of the Starches.	The rest.
Stork:	Introduction and up to the entrance of the Starches.	Prologue and after the entrance of the Starches, except perhaps the character of Simplicity.
Robb:	Same as Stork.	

There is nothing much to argue about here. The rhetoric and the buffoonery of the first part mark it clearly as Rowley's. So, too, do the hard words, of which there are at least half a dozen. The style of the last part—after the entrance of the Starches—is quite obviously Middleton's, and there are three Middleton parallels:

643–44:
> When we go to't and our fell ordnance play,
> 'Tis like the figure of a latter day.

Cf. *Hengist*, V.ii.3–4:
> That his destruction may appeare to him
> Ith figure of heauens wrath at ye Last day.

791–95:
> Thou foul eclipse, that, interposing equity,
> As the dark earth the moon, mak'st the world judge
> That blackness and corruption have possess'd
> The silver shine of justice, when 'tis only
> The smoke ascending from thy poisonous ways.

Cf. *Game at Chess*, IV.iv.54–57:
> Thick Darkness Dwells uppon this hower, Integritie
> (Like one of heauens bright luminaries now
> By Errors dullest Element interposde)
> Suffers a black Eclips.

850–51:
> Spots in deformèd faces are scarce noted,
> Fair cheeks are stain'd if ne'er so little blotted.

Cf. *Triumphs of Truth*, VII, 238, where the same couplet occurs.

Why Stork gives Rowley the character of Simplicity, unless he thinks that all clowns are Rowley's, I am at a loss to say. Simplicity's prose, in the introduction as well as in the text, seems to me Middleton's. Stork may well be right about the prologue, though the evidence is not very definite.

1620
The Marriage of the Old and New Testament

Authorship: The dedication is signed by Middleton.

1621
Honorable Entertainments

See Bentley, IV, 879–81, and the reprint in the Malone Society Reprints, ed. R. C. Bald, Oxford, 1953.

1621
The Sun in Aries

See Bentley, IV, 895–96.

c. 1621
Anything for a Quiet Life

See Bentley, IV, 859–61, where the literature on authorship is listed.

Bullen: "I suspect that the play in its present shape has been revised by another hand. The character of Lady Cressingham is drawn very much in the manner of Shirley. . . . Perhaps Middleton left the play unfinished and Shirley completed it."

Sykes: Webster: "Practically the whole of" I; II.i; III.i; IV.i, ii (dialogue between Knavesby and his wife at the beginning); and V.i–ii (V.i in Bullen). Webster and Middleton: V.iii (V.ii in Bullen). Middleton: Subsidiary action.

Lucas: Same as Sykes, except that he finds some traces of Webster in III.ii.

Oliphant: Same as Sykes, except that he gives Middleton III.i, the whole of IV.ii, and V.i (before George's entrance), and Webster III.ii (after Sweetball's exit).

Dunkel: Webster can at most have revised the play, which is substantially Middleton's.

Bentley: "No significant evidence has been presented that Webster had anything to do with *Anything for a Quiet Life*."

Dyce noticed that the phrase "the wild benefits of nature" (IV.i.89–90) occurs in both the *Arcadia* and *The Duchess of Malfi*, but it was left for Sykes to show that Webster had a substantial share in the play. His evidence—his most convincing evidence at least—consists of parallels with Webster's other plays (including *The Fair Maid of the Inn*), with Sidney's *Arcadia* (from which Webster often borrowed), and with the 1615 additions to Overbury's *Characters* (of which Webster was probably the author). Lucas adds parallels and gives besides a table of metrical evidence. Despite Bentley, I cannot help feeling that the case for Webster is a strong one. In any event, I am quite convinced —by the metrical evidence if by nothing else—that Middleton was not the sole author of the play.

My own division differs very slightly from that of Sykes listed above: Middleton: II.ii–iv; III.ii; IV.ii–iii. Webster: I; II.i; III.i; IV.i; V.i–ii. There may be some Webster in III.ii and IV.ii, some Middleton in V.ii.

1622
An Invention for the Lord Mayor

See Bentley, IV, 882.

1622
The Changeling

See Bentley, IV, 861–64, and, for authorship, Schoenbaum, pp. 208–17. My own division, given by Schoenbaum, is Middleton: II.i–ii; III.i–ii, iv; IV.i–ii; V.i–ii; Rowley: I; III.iii; IV.iii; V.iii. There is, however, a possibility that Middleton was concerned in IV.iii; see C. L. Barber, "A Rare Use of the Word *Honour* as a Criterion of Middleton's Authorship," *English Studies,* XXXVIII (August, 1957), 161–68.

1622
The Triumphs of Honor and Virtue

See Bentley, IV, 897–98.

1623
Lines Prefixed to "The Duchess of Malfi"

1623
The Triumphs of Integrity

See Bentley, IV, 898–99.

1624
A Game at Chess

See Bentley, IV, 870–79.

1626
The Triumphs of Health and Prosperity

See Bentley, IV, 896–97.

>1627
Women Beware Women

See Bentley, IV, 905–7.
Date: In "The Date of Middleton's *Women Beware Women,*" *Philological Quarterly,* XXII (October, 1943), 338–42, Baldwin

Maxwell finds an allusion to the sixty women who in 1621 were sent to Virginia as wives for the colonists, but Miss Jacobs (whose dissertation is listed by Bentley) shows that other women were sent to Virginia. Thus the allusion is at best doubtful.

LOST WORKS

1602
Caesar's Fall; or Two Shapes

With Dekker, Drayton, Munday, and Webster. See Henslowe, *Diary*, ed. W. W. Greg (London, 1904–8), I, 166, 167; II, 222.

1602
The Chester Tragedy; or Randal Earl of Chester

See Henslowe, *Diary*, I, 171; II, 225.

1602
Unnamed play

See Henslowe, *Diary*, I, 182; II, 232.

1606
The Viper and Her Brood

See Harold N. Hillebrand, "Thomas Middleton's *The Viper's Brood*," *Modern Language Notes*, XLII (January, 1927), 35–38.

1614
The Masque of Cupid

See Dyce, I, xix–xx.

1626
Unnamed and unacted pageant for the entry of the King and Queen

See Robert Withington, *English Pageantry* (Cambridge and London, 1918–20), I, 234–35, and Bentley, IV, 911.

(?)

The Puritan Maid, the Modest Wife, and
the Wanton Widow

Entered in the S. R. for Moseley, September 9, 1653. See Bentley, IV, 892.

(?)

The Conqueror's Custom; or the Fair
Prisoner

Listed in British Museum, Add. MS. 2893. See Bentley, IV, 864–66.

WORKS ATTRIBUTED TO MIDDLETON

1601–2

Blurt, Master Constable; or the Spaniard's
Night-Walk

See Chambers, III, 439.

Authorship: See E. H. C. Oliphant, "The Authorship of 'The Revenger's Tragedy,'" *Studies in Philology*, XXIII (April, 1926), 166; Mark Eccles, "Middleton's Birth and Education," *Review of English Studies*, VII (October, 1931), 434; R. C. Bald, "The Chronology of Middleton's Plays," *Modern Language Review*, XXXII (January, 1937), 34; J. G. McManaway, "Latin Title-Page Mottoes as a Clue to Dramatic Authorship," *Library*, 4th Series, XXVI (June, 1945), 28–36; Danied B. Dodson, Thomas Middleton's City Comedies (unpublished Columbia dissertation, 1954), pp. 11–38.

In 1661 Kirkman ascribed the play to Middleton, and the ascription was generally accepted until 1926, when—in the course of an article on *The Revenger's Tragedy*—Oliphant casually remarked that it seemed to him the work of Thomas Dekker. In 1931 Eccles gave several reasons for believing that Oliphant was right, and in 1937 Bald gave further reasons for thinking that Middleton was not the author of the play. These reasons, which, with a few others, I have tried to summarize below, make it impossible to include the play in the canon of Middleton's work.

Eccles remarks that the characters of Violetta and Imperia can only have been drawn by Dekker. This is quite true. Violetta is a romantic heroine like Caelestine in *Satiromastix* and Infelice in *The Honest Whore;* there are no romantic heroines in Middleton. Imperia is a sympathetic portrait of a courtesan, drawn with great delicacy and a high degree of imagination. In some respects she resembles Bellafront, particularly in the first scene in which she appears; but she is quite unlike the unscrupulous courtesans of Middleton's city comedies. The pages Doyt, Dandyprat, Truepenny, and Pilcher and the servant Frisco are also characters who are very much in Dekker's manner.

Middleton's plays are usually well constructed; Dekker's are not—they drift from episode to episode and are sometimes completely incoherent. *Satiromastix* is an extreme example, but it is scarcely more incoherent than *Blurt*, in which the central episode is not even clear. A. W. Ward (*A History of English Dramatic Literature*, London, 1875, II, 74) severely reprimands the author for permitting his hero to be unfaithful, and Bullen (I, xxi–iii) reprimands Ward for misinterpreting the plot. The hero, Bullen says, merely seeks shelter at the courtesan's house, where, in fact, he has arranged to meet his bride. But from the text itself the reader has difficulty in determining which of the two critics is right.

The verse, Bald says, is too deliberately poetical for Middleton, the prose too self-consciously euphuistic. But it is perhaps possible to go farther than this and say that both the verse and the prose seem to be Dekker's. Long illustrations are not very satisfactory, because Dekker's inspiration seldom lasts through a speech of twenty or thirty lines. He is always at his best in fragments—in single sentences or even single phrases—where he seems to throw off entirely without effort his most brilliant and his most characteristic conceits. Here are a few fragments from *Blurt* set beside a few others from *Satiromastix*:

And of beauty what tongue would not speak the best, since it is the jewel that hangs upon the brow of heaven, the best colour that can be laid upon the cheek of earth?

Come, come, come, will you condemn the mute rushes to be pressed to death by your sweet body?

The god of rest
Play music to thine eyes!

Night, clap thy velvet hand
Upon all eyes!

. . . flowers neuer dye a sweeter death, than when they are smoother'd to death in a Louers bosome. . . .

for could we write on paper,
Made of these turning leaues of heauen, the cloudes. . . .

O stop that speedy messenger of death;
O let him not run downe that narrow path,
Which leades vnto thy heart.

Night and Sleepe,
With silken Ribands would tye vp our eyes.

Preciosity is perhaps the most striking quality in all of these passages, and it is quite as apparent in the first group as in the second. Clearly the plays from which the passages come might have been written by the same man.

Middleton, Bald shows, is not fond of local color, and he certainly uses none in *The Phoenix,* his only early comedy with a foreign setting. Yet there is a good deal of local color in *Blurt.* Bald mentions the courtesans, the name Imperia, and a number of specific passages. There are a good many chorus speeches in the play—far more than in any play known to have been written by Middleton. There are only a few examples of *in faith,* Middleton's favorite oath (none at all according to Dodson's count), but there are many examples of the oaths commonly used by Dekker. *God's lid, God's me, God's my life, udsfoot,* and *Ho God* are obvious illustrations. There are also oaths used for the purpose of local color—notably the *by Saint Mark* noticed by Bald—and oaths used for the purpose of characterization: Dekker often does this, Middleton seldom or never. Thus Imperia repeatedly swears *by my virginity;* she also uses such characteristic forms as *by the moist hand of love, by the panting pulse of Venus, by the light oath of my fan,* and *by my ventoy* (cf. *Satiromastix,* I, 241: *by my Fan*). Simperina swears *by my pure maidenhead* and *by the crown of my maidenhead* (cf. *1 Honest Whore,* III, 36: *I lay my little maidenhead*).

There are many images that are repeatedly used elsewhere in Dekker's work, as the image of hair standing on end, the image of conjuring, the image of summoning to a parley, and the image of hoisting sails. There are parallels, though I must say not very good ones. The following are examples:

II.ii.272–73:

I knew what hook would choke him, and therefore baited that for him to nibble upon.

Cf. *2 Honest Whore*, III, 187–88: I go a-fishing with these baits. She nibbled, but would not swallow the hook. Also *Whore of Babylon*, II, 234 (though you bait hookes with gold,/ Ten thousand may be nibbling, when none bites).

III.i.111–12:

But say a golden slumber chance to tie,
With silken strings the cover of love's eye.

Cf. *Satiromastix*, I, 264:

Night and *Sleepe*,
With silken Ribands would tye vp our eyes.

III.iii.62–63:

That is the . . . very cream of all, and therefore how to skim off that only.

Dodson compares *Wonderful Year*, I, 134: This was the creame of her confession, which being skimd off. . . .

V.ii.121–23:

I prithee, try mine eyes if they know him, that have almost drowned themselves in their own salt water.

Cf. *Wonderful Year*, I, 131: such thicke teares . . . that in their salt water, all his vtterance was drownd.

V.ii.134–35:

thou makest my little eyes smart with washing themselves in brine.

Cf. *2 Honest Whore*, III, 154: I should be well seasoned, for mine eyes lie in brine. Also *Westward Ho*, II, 336: I confesse I haue laid mine eyes in brine.

1604
The Meeting of Gallants at an Ordinary

Critical edition: Ed. by F. P. Wilson in Dekker, *Plague Pamphlets*, Oxford, 1925.

Authorship: Wilson, the only scholar to study *The Meeting of Gallants,* finds several parallels with Middleton's pamphlets, *The Ant and the Nightingale* and *The Black Book.* But he finds more parallels with Dekker's pamphlets, notably *News from Graves-End,* and he is inclined to think that the tone is Dekker's rather than Middleton's. "The tragical mirth of the tales is," he says on p. xx, "like that of *The Wonderfull yeare* and has no counterpart in T. M.'s work. The gusto is more genial, the satire more tolerant, and occasionally the comic and satirical intent of the writer gives place to a warmth of pity rarely to be found in the cutting irony of T. M."

c. 1605(?)
The Second Part of the Honest Whore

See Chambers, III, 294–95.

Authorship: Dyce includes the play in his edition of Middleton, and though Bullen does not, he says, in I, xxvi, that he recognizes Middleton's hand "in a few comic scenes of the Second Part." No evidence for Middleton has been presented, by Bullen or anyone else.

1604–6
The Puritan; or the Widow of Watling Street

See Chambers, IV, 41–42.

Date: Not earlier than 1604, because in III.v.160–61 there is an allusion to the Act against Witchcraft passed in that year. 1606 is the most likely date, as in III.v.290–92 July 15 is said to fall on Tuesday, as it did in 1606, and in IV.iii.90–91 there may be an allusion to *Macbeth.* See Baldwin Maxwell, *Studies in the Shakespeare Apocrypha* (New York, 1956), pp. 109–37.

Authorship: See Bullen, I, lxxix–xc; Mermaid *Middleton,* I, xxxiii–iv; Fleay, II, 92–93; Symons in the *Cambridge History of English Literature* (Cambridge, 1932), VI, 62; *The Shakespeare Apocrypha,* ed. C. F. Tucker Brooke (Oxford, 1908), pp. xxx–xxxiii; A. Tzeutschler, *Das Drama "The Puritan"* (Breslau, 1909), pp. 42–54; W. D. Dunkel, *The Dramatic Technique of*

Thomas Middleton (Chicago, 1925), Appendix I; Dunkel, "The Authorship of *The Puritan*," *PMLA*, XLV (September, 1930), 804–8; Mark Eccles, "Middleton's Birth and Education," *Review of English Studies*, VII (October, 1931), 437–39.

Despite the "W. S." of the title-page, the play is certainly not Shakespeare's. Most modern authorities, including Bullen and Fleay, think that it is Middleton's; Dunkel and Eccles argue his case. Brooke objects on the ground that I.ii can have been written only by an Oxford man; he suggests Marston, or perhaps Marston, Jonson, and Chapman, since he feels that the play resembles *Eastward Ho*. But it is now known that Middleton, like Marston, was educated at Oxford. Swinburne and Symons object on the more reasonable ground that the play is too bad for Middleton. It is not, however, much worse than his earliest work, *The Family of Love*. Tzeutschler points out differences between *The Puritan* and Middleton's city drama.

Middleton is known to have written a play with a somewhat similar title, *The Puritan Maid, the Modest Wife, and the Wanton Widow*; see p. 196. But it can scarcely be identified with *The Puritan* or *The Puritan Widow*—both titles are used in the quarto —where there is no wanton widow but only a widow and her two daughters. In a general way *The Puritan* resembles Middleton's city comedies. It deals with London manners; it is decidedly picaresque. It contains passages of social protest like those in *The Ant and the Nightingale*—Eccles specifically mentions the passage about the Scholar; it contains passages ridiculing Puritans like those in *The Family of Love* and *A Chaste Maid in Cheapside*. It illustrates —in one scene at least—the kind of irony that Middleton habitually employs. But on the whole I think Swinburne is right: the play sounds less like Middleton than like Rowley or, more accurately, like a faithful disciple of Middleton's. It is difficult to imagine the author of *Michaelmas Term* turning out anything quite so primitive after, say, 1602 or 1603.

There is some stylistic evidence for Middleton. His favorite ejaculations, *pish* and *push*, are found in the play, and his favorite oath, *faith*, occurs in it with remarkable frequency. There are parallels of a sort, though not perhaps quite so many as one might expect even in a prose play.

I.i.6–7: Oh, I haue lost the deerest man, I haue buried the sweetest husband that euer lay by woman.
Tzeutschler compares *Michaelmas Term*, IV.iii.50–51: O master Rearage, I have lost the dearest husband that ever woman did enjoy!

I.i.159–60: how full of Aprill the poore soules eyes are!
Dunkel compares *Michaelmas Term*, IV.i.111–12: how pitiful my wife takes my death, which will appear by November in her eye. See also *Revenger's Tragedy*, V.i.161: teares like the Sunne in Aprill. But see too *Antony and Cleopatra*, III.ii.43: The April's in her eyes.

I.iv.299–300: I, by yon Beare at Bridge-Foote in heauen.
Dyce compares *No Wit*, V.i.267–68: the Bear at the Bridge-foot in heaven.

II.i.96–98: are not these Archers? what do you call 'em? Shooters: Shooters and Archers are all one, I hope.
Tzeutschler compares *No Wit*, II.i.24, 233–34, and III.i.78–79, where the same pun occurs.

III.iii.17–18: our doublets are buttond with Pewter.
Eccles compares *Ant and the Nightingale*, VIII, 83: shoulder-clapt by a pewter-buttoned sergeant. But Dekker has the same thing; see *Westward Ho*, II, 359: peuter-buttoned rascall; *Meeting of Gallants at an Ordinary*, p. 110: Pewter-buttonde Serieants.

III.v.287–90: *Pyeboord*. Stay, stay, stay. [*Pyeboord with an Almanack and the Captaine.*] *Captain*. Turne ouer, George. *Pyeboord*. Iune—Iulie: here, *Iulie*; thats this month.
Tzeutschler compares *No Wit*, I.i.259–62: *Weatherwise*. Stay, stay, stay! / What comfort gives my almanac to-day? [*Taking out an almanac.*] Luck, I beseech thee! [*Reads.*] *Good days, —evil days,—June,—July.* But Tzeutschler points out that both

passages may have been suggested by *Every Man Out of His Humor*, I.i.

V.ii.13–17: your Northen wench in her owne Countrie may well hold out till shee bee fifteene, but if she touch the South once, and come vp to *London*, here the Chimes go presently after twelue.

Eccles compares *Your Five Gallants*, I.i.166–67: Nay, I let twelve alone,/ For after twelve has struck, maids look for one. Also *Black Book*, VIII, 35: if her years have struck twelve once.

If the play could be dated a little earlier—if it could be regarded as one of Middleton's immature works—the stylistic evidence might perhaps be more convincing, but as it is, I think a reasonable doubt must remain. It may not be Middleton's after all.

1608
Timon of Athens

For authorship, see Schoenbaum, pp. 218–23.

1605–8
A Yorkshire Tragedy

See Chambers, IV, 54–55.

Authorship: See *The Shakespeare Apocrypha*, ed. C. F. Tucker Brooke (Oxford, 1908), pp. xxxiii–vi, and E. H. C. Oliphant, *The Plays of Beaumont and Fletcher* (New Haven, 1927), p. 457. The possibility that Middleton may have been the author of this play is suggested by Oliphant, but it is not a possibility that need be taken very seriously. There is, as far as I can see, no evidence for it at all.

1606–23
Macbeth

Date: The one given above is of course the date of the revision, which could have been carried out at any time between the original production of the play and the publication of the Shakespeare folio.

Authorship: See *Macbeth,* New Variorum Shakespeare, ed. H. H. Furness, 3d edition (Philadelphia, 1903), pp. 361–69; E. K. Chambers, *William Shakespeare, a Study of Facts and Problems* (Oxford, 1930), I, 472; *Macbeth,* ed. J. Dover Wilson (Cambridge, 1947), pp. xxiii–iv; J. M. Nosworthy, "The Hecate Scenes in *Macbeth,*" *Review of English Studies,* XXIV (April, 1948), 138–39; W. W. Greg, *The Shakespeare First Folio* (Oxford, 1955), p. 397, note E.

The connection between *Macbeth* and *The Witch* has been discussed since the eighteenth century. Steevens notices resemblances between the two plays and supposes that Shakespeare imitated Middleton. Clark and Wright list scenes and passages in *Macbeth*—a really formidable number of them—that they consider un-Shakespearean and suspect that the play was revised, "not improbably" by Middleton. Fleay is more certain of Middleton's presence and more liberal in assigning him passages. In recent years, however, scholars have become considerably more conservative. Chambers limits Middleton's share in the play to III.v and IV.i.39–43 and 125–32, and Dover Wilson adds to this no more than a few couplets. Nosworthy, one of the last in the field, is the most conservative of all. He is inclined to doubt that Middleton had any connection with the play whatsoever, and in the account that follows I have accepted this view.

The evidence for Middleton rests on the fact that two of his songs are introduced into the play. The first is announced in the stage directions following III.v.33 and 35 (*"Musicke, and a Song . . . . Sing within. Come away, come away, etc."*), and the second in the stage direction following IV.i.43 (*"Musicke and a Song. Blacke Spirits, etc."*). Both are clearly Middleton songs, written for *The Witch,* where indeed they are given in full. At some time between 1606 and 1623 the King's Men presumably felt that the operatic effects in Shakespeare's play could stand a little padding and used for the purpose material from an unsuccessful play of Middleton's. The two songs were part of the material and so was a dance—the one described in the stage direction following IV.i.132 (*"Musicke. The Witches Dance, and vanish"*).

Now the interpolations had to be introduced, and so three pieces of dialogue were written into the play. The first and longest, comprising the whole of III.v, introduces the new character of Hecate and leads up to "Come away, come away." The second begins with the stage direction, *"Enter Hecat, and the other three Witches,"* though three witches are already on the stage. The third consists of a speech by the First Witch, a lively one since the dance that it introduces was presumably lively.

The King's Men may well have hired Middleton to write the three pieces of dialogue. He was, after all, one of their regular dramatists and, in the years following Shakespeare's retirement, at least, the one presumably best fitted for the task. Still there is nothing to indicate that they did hire him and there is certainly nothing in the passages themselves that is in any way characteristic of him. The theories described above—in so far as they assign Middleton a share in the text—must be regarded as almost pure guesswork.

>1616(?)
The Nice Valor; or the Passionate Madman

See Bentley, III, 381–84.

Authorship: See Beaumont and Fletcher, *Works,* ed. Alexander Dyce (London, 1843–46), X, 295; R. Boyle, "Beaumont, Fletcher and Massinger," *Englische Studien,* VIII (1885), 53–54; Macaulay in the *Cambridge History of English Literature* (Cambridge, 1932), VI, 140; Fleay, I, 196–97; C. M. Gayley, *Beaumont, the Dramatist* (New York, 1914), p. 378; M. Chelli, *Étude sur la collaboration de Massinger avec Fletcher et son groupe* (Paris, 1926), p. 306; E. H. C. Oliphant, *The Plays of Beaumont and Fletcher* (New Haven, 1927), pp. 439–51.

Dyce:	Fletcher and another.
Boyle:	Fletcher, revised by Rowley.
Fleay:	Fletcher and another; revised, perhaps by Middleton.
Macaulay:	Fletcher and another, possibly Rowley.
Gayley:	No Beaumont in the play.
Chelli:	Fletcher and another.
Sykes:	At least partly Middleton.
Wells:	Mostly Middleton.
Oliphant:	Some Beaumont and Fletcher but mostly Middleton.

The external evidence is about the same as it is for *Wit at Several Weapons*. The play was entered in the S. R. as Beaumont and Fletcher's, published in the folio of their work, and ascribed to them by Archer. Both the prologue and the epilogue, however, speak of "Our Poet"; the first seems to refer to Fletcher and the second to Beaumont. Immediately following the play in the folio is Beaumont's *Letter to Ben Jonson*, written—so the heading says—"before he and Mr. *Fletcher* came to *London*, with two of the precedent Comedies then not finish'd." *The Nice Valor* might conceivably be one of the comedies in question.

Much of the internal evidence also points to Beaumont or Fletcher or both. The play is an example—a particularly flagrant example, in fact—of the kind of aristocratic drama that they specially cultivated. The chief character is a hopeless snob with a preposterously refined sense of honor; Middleton could by no stretch of the imagination have drawn him, but Beaumont or Fletcher might easily have done so. Yet the style of the play often is, or seems to be, Middleton's. Images characteristic of him repeatedly occur in the dialogue, and one sometimes seems to get the full flavor of his verse.

> Oh, I am so careful where I reverence,
> So just to goodness, and her precious purity,
> I'm as equally jealous, and as fearful,
> That any undeserved stain might fall
> Upon her sanctified whiteness, as of the sin
> That comes by wilfulness.   X, 149

> Oh the noblest welcome
> That ever came from man, meet thy deservings:
> Methinks I've all joyes treasure in mine arms now.   X, 152

If lines such as these are not Middleton's they were certainly written by a person familiar with his work.

How is one to explain the difference between the content and the style? Possibly, as Oliphant and others have done, by a theory of revision. Oliphant supposes that the play was originally written by Beaumont, later revised by Fletcher, and later still revised again by Middleton. The theory covers the facts well enough, but there is unfortunately not enough objective evidence to support it. One can scarcely be sure of Beaumont merely because he might have conceived the characters, and one can scarcely be sure of Middleton merely because some of the verse sounds like his.

1623
The Spanish Gipsy

See Bentley, IV, 892–95.

Authorship: See Dyce, I, lv; Bullen, I, lxxii; Mermaid *Middleton*, I, xxx–xxxi; Fleay, II, 101–2; Wiggin, pp. 40–42; *The Spanish Gipsie* and *All's Lost by Lust*, ed. E. C. Morris, Belles Lettres Series (Boston and London, 1908), introduction; Stork, pp. 41–43; H. Dugdale Sykes, *Sidelights on Elizabethan Drama* (London, 1924), pp. 183–99; E. H. C. Oliphant, *Shakespeare and His Fellow Dramatists* (New York, 1929), II, 18; W. D. Dunkel, "Did Not Rowley Merely Revise Middleton?" *PMLA*, XLVIII (September, 1933), 799–805; M. Joan Sargeaunt, *John Ford* (Oxford, 1935), pp. 41–57; U. M. Ellis-Fermor, *The Jacobean Drama* (London, 1936), p. 151, note; H. J. Oliver, *The Problem of John Ford* (Melbourne, 1955), pp. 29–34.

	Middleton	Rowley
Dyce:	Clara and Constanza beyond the ability of R.	—
Bullen:	—	Gipsy scenes doubtless largely his work.
Swinburne:	"Whatever is best in the tragic or in the romantic part."	May be traced "in many of the most animated scenes."
Fleay:	Whole play.	"Touched up" M.'s work.
Wiggin:	"Greater part."	Act II.
Morris:	Original author.	Revised the serious parts; "completely rephrased the comedy parts."
Stork:	The rest.	I (part); II; III (Sancho and Soto); IV.i; V (end).
Sykes:	"Substantially, if not wholly, from the pen of John Ford."	
Oliphant:	"Seems in the main to be from the workshop of Ford and Dekker; but there are also a few uncertain signs of Middleton."	

Dunkel:	Middleton wrote the play; Rowley and perhaps Ford revised it.
Sargeaunt:	Main plot: Ford. Gipsy scenes: collaborator.
Ellis-Fermor:	Ford possibly collaborated with Middleton.
Bentley:	"No persuasive evidence to contradict the normal assumption that the play was an ordinary collaboration between Middleton and Rowley."
Oliver:	Same as Ellis-Fermor.

My own feeling is that Sykes is right, but in any case I think I can safely say that the play never reads like Middleton. The style is sometimes precious, as in "Thou lady regent of the air, the moon" and "She greets me with a bracelet of her tears," and sometimes extremely simple, as in Clara's speech after her violation:

> Live a new man: if e'er you marry—
> O me, my heart's a-breaking!—but if e'er
> You marry, in a constant love to her
> That shall be then your wife, redeem the fault
> Of my undoing. I am lost for ever:
> Pray, use no more words.   I.iii.96–101

These lines, as Miss Sargeaunt says, can be set beside the most moving and most characteristic lines of Ford.

The last scholars in the field often seem particularly persuasive, but this is scarcely the case here. Bentley refuses to examine the evidence in detail, and Oliver, after judiciously reviewing the evidence for Ford, remarks "that Middleton, the chameleon dramatist if ever there was one, is always likely to imitate someone else's style perfectly." I find this an astounding statement.

(?)
The Bloody Banquet

See Bentley, III, 282–84.

Authorship: See Schoenbaum, pp. 223–26. The case for Middleton is very tenuous indeed.

Index